Killer Whales

# Killer Whales

John K.B. Ford, Graeme M. Ellis, and Kenneth C. Balcomb

**The natural history**

**and genealogy of**

***Orcinus orca* in**

**British Columbia and**

**Washington State**

*UBC Press / Vancouver*

*University of Washington Press / Seattle*

Printed in Canada on acid-free paper ∞

ISBN 0-7748-0469-6

**Canadian Cataloguing in Publication Data**

Ford, John Kenneth Baker, 1955-
    Killer whales

    ISBN 0-7748-0469-6

    1. Killer whale – British Columbia. 2. Killer whale – Washington (State). I. Ellis, Graeme, 1950-. II. Balcomb, Kenneth C., 1940- . III. Title.

QL737.C432F67 1994    599.5'3    C94-910346-2

UBC Press gratefully acknowledges the ongoing support to its publishing program from the Canada Council, the Province of British Columbia Cultural Services Branch, and the Department of Communications of the Government of Canada.

UBC Press
University of British Columbia
6344 Memorial Road
Vancouver, BC V6T 1Z2
(604) 822-3259
Fax: (604) 822-6083

Published simultaneously in the United States of America by the University of Washington Press, P.O. Box 50096, Seattle, WA 98145-5096

**Library of Congress Cataloging-in-Publication Data**

Ford, John K.B.
    Killer whales: the natural history and genealogy of Orcinus orca in British Columbia and Washington State / John K.B. Ford, Graeme Ellis, and Kenneth C. Balcomb.
        p.    cm.
    Includes bibliographic references.
    ISBN 0-295-97396-X
    1. Killer whale – British Columbia. 2. Killer whale – Washington (State). I. Ellis, Graeme M. II. Balcomb, Kenneth C., 1940- . III. Title.

QL737.C432F67        1994                    94-18023
599.5'3 – dc20                                CIP

Published in cooperation with the Vancouver Aquarium; the Pacific Biological Station, Department of Fisheries and Oceans, Nanaimo, BC; and the Center for Whale Research, Friday Harbor, WA

*We dedicate this book*
*to the memory of Michael Bigg,*
*our friend and mentor.*

# Contents

This book has its beginnings in the early 1970s. At that time, the late Dr. Michael Bigg, Ian MacAskie, and one of us (Graeme Ellis), working at the Pacific Biological Station in Nanaimo, British Columbia, were studying the population status of killer whales in the province. This proved to be no small task. Conventional census techniques, such as aerial or vessel transect surveys, were not practical because of the vastness of the convoluted British Columbia coastline and the wide-ranging distribution of the whales. A public sighting program using mail-in questionnaires yielded a very rough estimate of the population size, but nothing about birth and death rates, social organization, and other vital aspects of the whales' life history. Clearly another study technique was needed.

By 1973, Mike Bigg, always the inventor and innovator, had discovered a technique that was to revolutionize field studies of killer whales on this coast and, in the future, in other regions of the world. Mike realized that the whales were all carrying natural markings on their bodies and that these could be used for the cetacean equivalent of a mug-shot identification system. All one had to do was obtain a good photograph of the dorsal fin and grey "saddle" patch at the base of the fin, and the whale could be identified from the unique pattern of nicks and scars. Mike reasoned that if every individual present during repeated encounters with whale groups along the coast was photographically identified, the population could actually be counted rather than estimated, and many other features of the species' natural history could be examined. Many scientists were sceptical about the validity of this new approach, but Mike persisted and demonstrated that photo-identification was indeed the key to understanding this species.

The study continued through the 1970s and expanded as other researchers joined the collaborative effort. Two of us became involved during this period. In 1976, Ken Balcomb formed a research group on San Juan Island and started an intensive multifaceted study of the portion of the population that frequents US waters. This research program, operated by the Center for Whale Research, continues today. In 1977, John Ford began graduate studies at the University of British Columbia, focusing on the underwater vocalizations of the whales and their relationship to behaviour and social structure. This work also continues today.

By the early 1980s, our understanding of the coastal killer whales and our relationship with them began to enter a new era. Scientifically, a most remarkable picture was emerging. Killer whales were far from conventional mammals; indeed, certain aspects of their biology appeared unique. Two different forms of the species – residents and transients – lived in the same waters, yet never associated and seemed to specialize on different prey – fish for residents and mammals for transients. The social structure of the resident whales was exceptionally unusual, with young whales staying in their mother's group well into maturity and probably for their entire lives. Also, each resident killer whale pod was found to have a unique vocal dialect that appeared to encode its relationship to other pods in the population.

During this period, the whales were attracting the attention of more than just researchers. Plans to turn Robson Bight, a sheltered bay on northeastern Vancouver Island, into a log-booming area threatened this important whale habitat. Lobbying efforts by conservationists eventually led to the creation of an ecological reserve for the whales in Robson Bight in 1982, and, in the process, the area became widely known as the best place for the public to view killer whales in the wild. The opening of a road to northern Vancouver Island in 1979 improved access to the area, and Johnstone Strait quickly grew in popularity as a destination for recreational whale watching from private boats and kayaks. In 1980 the first commercial whale-watching excursions began in the Strait, and soon people were travelling from throughout North America and abroad to watch killer whales in British Columbia.

As interest in recreational whale watching continued to grow, both in British Columbia and Washington State, so too did the demand from whale enthusiasts for a book containing the latest information on killer whale natural history and a catalogue of photographs to identify individual whales and their family groups. Such a book was co-authored and published in 1987 by Mike Bigg and the three of us, but it was very much Mike Bigg's project. Mike was the pioneer of modern killer whale research, and it was his enthusiasm, cooperative spirit, and love for the animals that was responsible for much of the success of the scientific work, as well as this first book on killer whale natural history and identification. Mike hoped that the book would be updated every four to five years as the population changed and new discoveries were made, and that this might "result in the killer whales of this region becoming one of the best understood of all marine mammals."

Sadly, Mike Bigg was not to live to see the next edition of his book. In October 1990, Mike passed away at the age of 51, leaving many friends and students to carry on the work that was so important to him.

We have tried to prepare this second edition of the book with the same spirit that Mike Bigg would have put into it. Much has changed since 1987. There have been a number of new findings in the ongoing research. Many of the females born at the start of the study are now producing their first offspring. Males that were subadult in 1987 have "sprouted" (see glossary), and their dorsal fins do not resemble those shown in the earlier catalogue. The population of identified killer whales on the coasts of British Columbia and Washington has jumped from about 350 to almost 600 with the discovery of a new community of "offshore" killer whales. The resident population itself has grown from 255 in 1987 to 305 in 1993, despite some 19 whales known or suspected to have died during the same period. With such a large number of whales now known, we decided that it would be impractical to include them all in the photographic registry in this book. Thus, although we discuss the natural history of resident, transient, and offshore killer whales, only the residents are included in the catalogue, as these are by far the most commonly encountered whales in coastal waters. (We plan to publish a separate catalogue of transient and offshore killer whales in the future.) Most descriptive sections have been modified and updated, but one, "The Development of Our Study," we have left as Mike Bigg wrote it.

Like its predecessor, this book is the product of countless people, too numerous to list here. As mentioned in the first edition, the study has involved several thousand people who called us to report whale sightings and over 200 people who took photographs that were used to document whales. For ongoing contribution of identification photographs and/or acoustical recordings, sharing of data and ideas, or other special assistance we thank the following: Dave Arcese, David Bain, Robin Baird, Kelley Balcomb-Bartok, Lance Barrett-Lennard, Anne Borrowman, Jim Borrowman, David Briggs, John Brouwer, Randy Burke, Diane Claridge, Jim Darling, John De Boeck, David Ellifrit, Dave Duffins, Brian Falconer, Beverly Ford, Pat Gerlach, Dawn Goley, Nancy Haenel, Elvira Harms, Jim and Sara Heimlich-Boran, Kathy Heise, Jeff Jacobsen, Ian MacAskie, Bill and Donna Mackay, Rod MacVicar, John McCulloch, Bill McIntyre, Craig Matkin, Alex Morton, Linda Nichol, Peter Olesiuk, Rich Osborne, Rod Palm, Naomi Rose, Leah Saville, Paul Spong, Pam Stacey, Helena Symonds, Astrid van Ginneken, Jane Watson, Eugene White, and Steve Wischniowski.

We are grateful to the following organizations for their continuing financial support of this work: Pacific Biological Station, Department of Fisheries and Oceans; Vancouver Aquarium; Stubbs Island Whale Watching; West Coast Whale Research Foundation; Earthwatch; the Whale Museum; Parks Canada; Langara Fishing Lodge; PepsiCo Foundation; Confidence Foundation; and Island Foundation.

Many worked hard to help make this book a reality. Elwood Miles processed and printed the black-and-white photographs with great skill and care. George Vaitkunas digitally scanned the photographs, developed the layout, and designed the book. We especially thank Robin Taylor for her enthusiasm, organizational and editing skills, and her long-term commitment to the killer whales of British Columbia. Dean Fisher, Bev Ford, Valerie Shore, Andrew Trites, and Jane Watson reviewed earlier drafts and made many helpful comments.

# Our Changing Relationship with the Killer Whale

The killer whale, *Orcinus orca*, is second only to humans as the most widely distributed mammal on earth. It ranges from the tropical seas through the temperate zones to the edge of the pack ice at both poles. Yet it is only in the last quarter-century that we have begun to learn something about the nature of this remarkable animal. There are several reasons for this. Like all cetaceans (whales, dolphins, and porpoises), killer whales live at sea and spend most of their time underwater and out of sight. Compared to most terrestrial animals, this makes them difficult to observe and study in the wild. Also, the species does not appear to be very abundant in most parts of its range. There are concentrations in certain waters, such as off Antarctica, northern Japan, Iceland, Norway, Alaska, and British Columbia, but killer whales are only sighted sporadically in most parts of the world.

For many years, widespread fear and hatred of the animal also impeded an understanding of killer whale natural history. From ancient times, the killer whale featured prominently in marine folklore as a blood-thirsty, voracious predator that was extremely dangerous to humans. In the first century AD, the Roman scholar Pliny the Elder wrote, "A killer whale cannot be properly depicted or described except as an enormous mass of flesh armed with savage teeth." More recently, in 1874, the whaler Captain Charles Scammon wrote that "in whatever quarter of the world [killer whales] are found, they seem always intent upon seeking something to destroy or devour." Even as late as 1973, US Navy diving manuals described the killer whale as "extremely ferocious," warning that it "will attack human beings at every opportunity."

But killer whales have not been universally disliked throughout history. Native peoples of coastal regions in many parts of the world regarded the killer whale with awe and respect rather than hostility. Along the northwest coast of North America, Native cultures held the killer whale in high esteem, and it was featured prominently in their art and mythology. The Tlingit of southeast Alaska, for example, believed that the killer whale would never harm humans, but instead would aid them with gifts of strength, health, and food from

## Killer Whales as Nuisances

Killer whales have not always been well liked in British Columbia. In the late 1950s, perceived competition with sports fishermen for salmon, in addition to the general fear of the whales, led to plans by the Federal Department of Fisheries to reduce the number of killer whales in the Campbell River area. The following letter, dated 28 July 1960, is from a report by the committee planning this program:

*It is recommended that one .50 calibre machine gun with tripod mounting be used [at Seymour Narrows] with ball ammunition only ... If the whales approach from the westward, the method of attack would be to open fire when they approach ... in an endeavour to turn the herd back and so prevent them from entering Seymour Narrows and continuing on to the Campbell River area ... Should the whales approach from the Campbell River side, it would be preferable to withhold fire until they have passed to the westward of the gun position, to prevent turning back toward Campbell River.*

the sea, of which the killer whale was custodian. Killer whales remain an important component of Native traditions today.

Killer whales have long been viewed with particular animosity by fishermen, who regarded the whales as threats to their lives as well as their livelihood. In Norway, it was feared that killer whales were decimating herring stocks, so the government encouraged hunting of the species by whalers, even subsidizing this hunt in some years. Between 1938 and 1980, an average of 57 killer whales were taken each year. In British Columbia, fishermen also considered the whales to be nuisances and unfair competition, and they were frequently shot on sight. About 25% of the killer whales live-captured during the late 1960s and early 1970s carried evidence of having been previously shot and wounded. In 1960, under pressure from sports fishing lodges in the Campbell River area on Vancouver Island, the Federal Fisheries Department in 1960 developed a program to reduce killer whales by shooting them from a land-based machine gun. Although the gun was mounted, it was never fired; fortunately, the whales had shifted their foraging pattern to areas outside of Campbell River when the culling program was about to begin.

Killer whales have also been taken in some parts of the world for their meat and oil, usually as a by-catch of whaling operations focused on other species. The former USSR typically captured about 25 per season in their Southern Hemisphere whaling operations; then, in the 1979-80 whaling season, they took an unprecedented 916 whales. This raised concern among conservationists, and in 1982 the International Whaling Commission recommended against further killing until more was known about the impact on populations.

Attitudes towards and awareness of killer whales among the general public finally began to improve in the late 1960s. By then, a number of killer whales were being displayed in aquaria around the world, and millions of people were able to see for themselves that the animals were not the ferocious beasts of reputation. Instead, they were intelligent, inquisitive, and cooperative, as were their relatives, the smaller dolphins. This, combined with the emergence of an environmental

movement in North America in the 1970s, resulted in a new tolerance and compassion for the species. Interest in viewing killer whales in the wild soon developed, and the first commercial whale-watching excursions aimed at this species began in the Johnstone Strait area of British Columbia in 1980.

Today, killer whales are protected by many countries, and they are safe from exploitation in most parts of the world. None have been taken in commercial whaling operations anywhere since 1981. With the success of captive breeding, live captures for aquaria have become rare. Recreational killer whale watching has grown into a major pursuit, mostly in British Columbia and Washington State, but also to a lesser extent in Alaska and Norway. An estimated 25,000 people visited the Johnstone Strait area in 1993 to view the whales. Fresh bullet wounds are now rarely seen on whales in British Columbia and Washington State.

Coincidental with this new respect for the killer whale has come a new scientific understanding of the species. Field studies similar to our own are now under way in Alaska, Argentina, Norway, and the sub-Antarctic, and a fascinating story of this intelligent, innovative, and adaptable social predator is emerging. Killer whales have among the richest, most complex, social lives of any marine mammal. Some populations are made up of kin groups that are the most stable of any species, marine or terrestrial. Many of the whales' behaviour patterns, such as foraging specializations, appear to represent traditions that are passed on from generation to generation. Killer whales even have vocal dialects that define their social identity.

Every piece of knowledge that we gain about the killer whale compels us to learn more and adds to our deepening respect for this remarkable animal. Yet, just as we have entered this new era of compassion and understanding, we are threatening the whales in new, insidious ways. Pollution, over-fishing, and industrialization are all having an impact on the whales' habitat, and these pressures are increasing steadily. Only through awareness, understanding, and commitment – both within the public and scientific communities – can we succeed at preserving the whales' habitat and their future.

# The Development of Our Study

*The following section was written by the late Dr. Michael Bigg for our original catalogue, published in 1987. We have included it here, with only minor updating, as it best describes the history of killer whale research in British Columbia and Washington State.*

The study began in 1970. At that time, biologists in British Columbia and Washington State were faced with an urgent request. Fisheries managers and the public were concerned about the live-capturing of killer whales for aquaria. The commercial netting of these whales had begun in 1965 and grown rapidly. The questions posed concerned whether the removals were endangering the local killer whale population and what restrictions should be introduced if more whales were to be taken. This required knowing how many killer whales were in the region; whether the whales taken in Washington State were from the same stock as those taken in British Columbia; what the productivity of the population was; and whether the removal of one particular age or sex was detrimental to productivity. Little was known about these topics, and no method of data collection existed to obtain the answers.

We initiated field studies in 1971 by organizing a public sighting program to find out the approximate numbers of killer whales and where these whales could reliably be found. Questionnaires were sent to lighthouses, ferries, fishery patrol boats, tugs, fishermen, and other individuals who lived or worked along the coast of British Columbia. The method usually involves collecting sightings year-round. However, we modified it to take into account the problem of duplicate sightings of the same individuals seen at different locations. We asked sighters to watch on only a few specific days. A total of three censuses were conducted on 26 July 1971, 1-3 August 1972, and 1-2 August 1973, and 15,000 questionnaires were distributed for each. From the 500 or so returns each year, we estimated the population in British Columbia and Washington State at roughly 200-350 whales. This number was much lower than the many hundreds, and even thousands, that most people thought were present. The questionnaires in 1971-73 also indicated that western Johnstone Strait was the best location to study the species in British Columbia. Sighters reported that the whales could be found there during most days in summer.

For the 1972 field season, we went to Johnstone Strait during early August to observe the whales for ourselves. Killer whales were seen every day as expected, and we followed them around by boat, taking many photographs. The pictures revealed several individuals with distinctive nicks and gouges on their dorsal fins. This provided us with natural identification tags. If we could find these whales again, we would be able to learn about their daily lives.

We gambled that we could relocate the "tagged" whales and chartered two boats for studies in Johnstone Strait during August 1973. Within a few days we had found them, but more important, we found that many other individuals were also recognizable by their unique natural markings. The dorsal fin and the saddle patch, which is located at the base of the fin, varied in shape and often bore scars, indentations, and a wide variety of nicks and gouges. We had now discovered a method to study killer whales and could begin documenting the life histories of many individuals. With time we would be able to answer the management questions.

The study area expanded in 1974 to include eastern and southern Vancouver Island. However, unlike Johnstone Strait, we had the problem of how to reliably locate the whales on a daily basis. This was solved by borrowing a technique developed by the local killer whale netters. We organized a network of volunteer observers to call us whenever they saw killer whales, and we would then dispatch a boat and crew to find and photograph the whales.

The first task was to determine the number of killer whales in the region. To do this, we undertook an intensive census during 1-10 August 1974. Boats were stationed at seven strategic sites – Johnstone Strait, Campbell River, Stuart Island, Comox, Vancouver, Active Pass, and Victoria. Newspapers, radios, and marine broadcast stations were asked to announce that the census was in progress and to request that anyone sighting killer whales should immediately call a central dispatch number. The system worked well, and we managed to count all the resident whales off southern Vancouver Island, and most of those off northern Vancouver Island. During this period we saw no transient whales, but these are few in number and are seldom seen (see next section).

The study continued to expand over the next few years. Counts were conducted on a year-round basis off eastern and southern Vancouver Island. We went to Fitz Hugh Sound in August 1975, and in 1976 began what has since become an annual census in Washington State. In August 1978, we searched the Prince Rupert area. However, the study had clearly become too large by the late 1970s to carry out over such a wide area every year. This forced us to consolidate our efforts at two main sites, Johnstone Strait in British Columbia and Haro Strait in Washington State. It turns out that Haro Strait, like Johnstone Strait, has killer whales present almost every day in summer. All resident whales off British Columbia and Washington State usually visit one of these sites at some time each summer. Transient whales do not seem to have any particular site that they visit regularly.

The data-gathering routine has now become standardized. In Johnstone Strait, we locate the whales mainly by boat, often with the aid of a portable hydrophone. Other researchers, whale watchers, and boaters in the area also help to find them. In Haro Strait, they are located visually from the Center for Whale Research, on western San Juan Island. Early warning of their approach is received through a permanent hydrophone. A boat is then dispatched to intercept and photograph them. Whales are also reported by volunteer sighters living nearby along the waterfront.

The minimum information that we try to obtain from an encounter with a pod is the identity of all individuals present. We also attempt to determine the sex and travelling companions of each animal, and to make a tape recording of their vocalizations for studies of the different sounds made by each pod. Many other kinds of data can be collected, such as travel routes, group mixing, dive times, feeding activities, travel speeds, time spent on various activities, interactions with fishing operations, and so on.

In addition, we collect recordings from permanent hydrophones at Telegraph Cove and other locations, and audiotapes from other sites, such as at Orcalab on Hanson Island, are made available to us. From these, we can identify pods from their dialects. People maintaining the hydrophones often take photographs of the whales, which enable us to identify the individual whales that were present. We also receive photographs taken both by naturalists and the public, which are used to establish pod composition and distribution. We continue to search for historical photographs and tape recordings to help determine the ages of individual whales and to identify which pods were captured for aquaria during the late 1960s and early 1970s. Finally, we frequently exchange findings with the many researchers working on the species in this region.

We are now able to answer many of the original management questions. As a result of the years of data collection from various localities, information has been compiled on the population size, numbers of pods, pod composition, social organization, genealogy, movement patters, birth and death rates, feeding habits, breeding cycle, impact that captures for zoos and aquaria had on productivity of the population, and many other topics. Although these whales are no longer captured in British Columbia and Washington State, there are now new reasons for studying them. The beauty, size, and intelligence of killer whales makes us want to know more about their life cycle. With this unique research opportunity to look into their world, more can be learned about their society and their adaptations to life in the marine ecosystem. Understanding their biology will help ensure that killer whales will survive humankind's continuing encroachment.

# Natural History of the Killer Whale

One might expect that after twenty years of field research we would understand all of the important features of the life history and ecology of killer whales in British Columbia and Washington State. This, however, is far from the case. We and our colleagues have assembled a considerable amount of detailed information on certain aspects of the whales' biology, but answers to some fundamental questions have eluded us. Where are the whales in winter and what is their diet? Who are the fathers of the calves that we have seen born during the study? In the following sections, we will bring you up to date on what we know and don't know about the answers to such questions.

**Distinct Populations: Residents, Transients, and Offshores**

In the early stages of this study, we became accustomed to encountering killer whales in groups, or pods, containing 10 to 25 or more whales. These pods displayed certain characteristics that soon became familiar. Most of the time, individuals were dispersed singly or in small subgroups over a wide area, moving in the same direction but surfacing independently. Their movement patterns were fairly predictable, as was their occurrence in certain areas during the summer. Occasionally, however, small groups of killer whales were encountered that differed in appearance and behaviour from the larger pods. Typically the smaller groups contained only two to five whales, and their patterns of occurrence and movement were erratic. We found it curious that these small groups never travelled with the larger pods, and speculated that perhaps they were social outcasts in transit to other locations. For this reason, we termed the whales found in these small groups *transients* and those identified in the large, common pods *residents*.

Although we still do not fully understand the relationship between residents and transients, it is now clear that resident whales do not become transients, or vice versa. Instead, the two forms of killer whales are fundamentally different in most aspects of their behaviour, social organization, and ecology. We believe that these differences are so profound that the two forms are socially and genetically isolated, despite living in the same waters. One indicator of genetic differences between the two forms is the shape of the dorsal fin, which tends to be pointed at the tip in transients and rounded in residents, especially among mature females (see sidebar, p. 18). Preliminary genetic analysis of stranded or captive residents and transients indicates that the two forms are quite distinct, leading to speculation that they are separate subspecies on the evolutionary path towards becoming distinct species. Pending further genetic information, we consider them to be separate races.

Over the last few years, we have discovered what may be a third form of killer whale on the British Columbia coast, which we have provisionally designated as *offshores*. We have only had about twenty encounters with these whales and thus know little about them. Offshore killer whales tend to be found in large groups of 30 to 60 individuals, and are seldom seen in protected coastal waters. Most encounters have taken place near the Queen Charlotte Islands (Haida Gwaii) and 15 or more kilometres off the west coast of Vancouver Island. Although the ranges of residents, transients, and offshores overlap, they have never been seen to mix. We believe that the offshore whales may form a distinct race that spends most of its time on the continental shelf, feeding perhaps on schooling fish. It may be a decade or longer before we have a clearer picture of their natural history.

As of 1993, the resident killer whale population in British Columbia and Washington State was comprised of 305 whales. These individuals and the groups to which they belong are shown in the catalogue portion of this book. We are less sure of the population sizes for transients and offshores. A total of 170 transients have been identified in these coastal waters, but this may not represent the true population size. Many years may pass between re-sightings of individual transients, so we are uncertain about how many of these remain in this area or are alive today. Also, in most years we photograph several transients that were previously

■ Northern residents
■ Southern residents

### Distinguishing Resident, Transient, and Offshore Killer Whales

The dorsal fins of resident, transient, and offshore killer whales differ subtly in shape, especially in adult females. With a practised eye, it is possible to determine which form of whale you are seeing based on these differences, with the help of certain other clues. It is important to note, however, that the differences described here are not seen in every individual, but are typical of the majority for each form of killer whale.

In **residents**, the fin tip tends to be rounded and positioned over the rear insertion of the fin to the back. The leading edge of the fin tends to be straight or curved slightly back. Although the fin tip is generally rounded, this curve ends in a rather sharp angle at the rear corner of the tip. The grey "saddle patch" at the base of the fin may be either uniform in coloration or may contain various amounts of black – the latter known as "open saddles." Residents are usually seen in groups of 6 to 50 or more, and tend to surface at intervals of no more than 3-4 minutes.

The tip of the dorsal fin in **transient** females is typically pointed and positioned in the centre above the front and rear insertions of the fin. Also, the midpoint along the leading edge of the fin sometimes has a slight bulge. The saddle patch is typically quite large compared to residents and offshores, and open saddles are not found. Transients usually travel in groups of 6 or less, and often dive for periods of 5-7 minutes.

In most respects, the **offshore** form of killer whale is more similar to residents than to transients. The saddle patch is roughly the same relative size as that of residents, and open saddles are occasionally seen. The dorsal fin also tends to be rounded, although the shape of the tip often differs subtly. Rather than ending in a sharp angle at the rear corner of the tip, as in residents, the dorsal fin tends to be continuously rounded over the entire tip. Although there are no measurements available, the body size seems to be somewhat smaller than that of residents or transients. Offshores are usually seen in groups of 25 or more, and have diving characteristics not unlike those of residents.

*Dorsal fin has rounded tip, but usually with sharper angle at the rear corner*

*Dorsal fin tip generally pointed*

*Dorsal fin continuously rounded over tip, usually lacks the sharper angle at the rear corner*

**Resident fin**

*Open saddle, often seen in residents, occasionally in offshores, but not in any transients identified to date*

**Transient fin**

*Saddle patch large and uniformly grey*

**Offshore fin**

*Saddle patch either solid grey or open*

unidentified in the area. Similarly, we have little idea what the population size for offshore killer whales may be. Between 1989 and 1993, approximately 200 individuals have been identified, and each new encounter adds a number of new whales to the total.

### Different Lifestyles

The most important difference between residents and transients, and the one that influences all aspects of their distinctive lifestyles, is diet. Residents eat predominantly fish, while transients prefer marine mammal prey. Although we long suspected that these preferences existed for the two races, it is only during the last several years that we have realized how focused each form is on their respective prey. Early clues came from stranded whales. Residents that died and washed ashore typically had fish bones in their stomachs, while transient stomachs often contained hundreds of claws and whiskers of seals and sea lions, or pieces of porpoises. We have now logged many kills by each race, and these observations confirm the stomach contents data. Over 95% of resident kills we have observed were of salmon, with the remainder made up of other fish species. There are only a few examples of resident pods attacking seals or porpoises, but these involved harassments without any clear evidence of the whales actually eating the animals. Residents are often seen in the vicinity of other marine mammal species, but typically ignore them.

Transients, on the other hand, are very efficient marine mammal predators, but seem to ignore fish as a food source. More than one-half the kills we have documented were of harbour seals, followed by harbour and Dall's porpoises, and Steller and California sea lions. The transient predilection for warm-blooded prey extends beyond marine mammals. They will often harass and kill sea birds and occasionally eat them. There have also been several observations of unidentified killer whales – almost certainly transients – harassing or feeding on deer and, on one occasion, moose. These terrestrial mammals regularly swim narrow channels along the

Inside Passage, and may fall victim to transients more often than one might expect.

The different prey preferences of resident and transient killer whales dictate different foraging strategies and therefore different group sizes and structures. The social system of transients is much more fluid than the stable associations of residents. A typical transient group might be comprised of a mother and two or three offspring, or perhaps several adult females of unknown relationship. Some offspring leave their mother's group as adolescents, often following the birth of a younger sibling. Adult males, or bulls, often travel alone but may team up occasionally with other transients to form temporary foraging groups. Bulls are seldom found travelling solely with other adult males. Residents, on the other hand, tend to live in stable groups comprised of several related females and their young. Offspring of both sexes stay with their mother as long as she is alive, with the result that resident pods are often large and may simultaneously contain three or four generations. This social system is very unusual, not only among whales, but among mammals generally (see "Resident Killer Whale Societies," pp. 23-26, for more details).

Resident pods specialize on salmon for most of the year, and the whales' movement patterns coincide with the distribution and timing of salmon migrations. For example, northern residents congregate in the western Johnstone Strait area starting in mid-June, when the first salmon begin arriving on their migration to various rivers and streams, especially the Fraser River. The whales are very common here until late fall, when the last salmon runs pass through the area. When foraging for salmon, resident pods spread out and form a broad front that sweeps along the narrow coastal passages, often from shore to shore. They usually forage in a predictable fashion, moving from one good feeding spot to another. By exchanging underwater vocalizations, pod members keep in contact and possibly alert each other to the presence of prey. The whales produce rapid series of clicks that are used for echolocation of salmon and for navigation. Once a fish is detected, it is usually captured and eaten by individuals, or

1

2

1. Transient killer whales can reach speeds of over 20 knots when chasing prey. This transient, photographed at Chatham Point on Vancouver Island, made several high leaps through the air while attacking a Dall's porpoise, seen as a small burst of spray ahead of the whale.

2. Resident killer whales also show impressive bursts of speed while pursuing salmon prey. Here, the bull A32 (A1 pod) is chasing a chinook salmon along a rocky shoreline on the central BC coast.

1

2

3

occasionally a mother and her young offspring. Living in large pods may benefit each whale by increasing the overall success rate of locating scattered salmon. Making a living on salmon undoubtedly requires specialized knowledge that is passed on from generation to generation, and a whale's survival is enhanced by staying with its pod and taking advantage of these behavioural traditions.

Transient whales employ a very different foraging strategy for their marine mammal prey. Unlike residents, their movements are quite unpredictable. Travelling in small groups, transients roam widely, entering small coves, bays, and channels in search of seals, sea lions, or porpoises. They often dive for more than five minutes, and occasionally in excess of fifteen minutes (residents are seldom underwater for more than three to four minutes at a time). Transients seem to employ a "sneak attack" technique when hunting. Unlike residents, transient groups almost always forage in silence, probably to avoid detection by their acoustically alert mammalian prey. This is even true for echolocation clicks, which would help locate prey but would reveal the whales' presence. Instead, the transients appear to find prey by "passive sonar" – listening for the sounds made by the mammals they are hunting. Transients only vocalize freely once they are in the process of killing or eating prey. Members of a transient group will frequently cooperate to kill a marine mammal, especially the large and physically powerful sea lions. The tail flukes are first used to strike and stun the prey, and then it is drowned. Once killed, the mammal is often shared among group members.

How the newly discovered offshore killer whales may fit into this fish vs. mammal diet dichotomy is not yet clear. In many respects, they resemble residents, and we believe that they prey on salmon at least part of the year. They are frequently vocal, and use a great deal of echolocation, which suggests that they are primarily fish feeders. The large groups that the offshores tend to form also points to a piscivorous lifestyle. However, the possibility that they also take marine mammals cannot be ruled out.

*1. A transient whale rams a Steller sea lion from below. During such attacks, transients may ram or strike their prey with their tail flukes for an hour or more before it is drowned and eaten.*

*2. A southern resident whale with a half-eaten salmon.*

*3. A foraging northern resident male, probably in the process of catching a salmon, surprises a lone fisherman.*

## Dialects and Population Identity

Different killer whale populations can be distinguished by the kinds of underwater communication sounds they produce. These vocal variations, known as *dialects*, can provide important clues about the relationships of groups and populations. Like other toothed whales, killer whales produce a wide variety of acoustic signals that serve various purposes. Rapid series of clicks, mentioned earlier, are used as echolocation or sonar signals for navigation and detection of objects in the whale's surroundings. Other kinds of sounds, mostly whistles and burst-pulsed signals that resemble squeals, squawks, and screams, are used for social communication within and between groups. A large proportion of the social sounds of killer whales are quite stereotyped and distinctive in structure. Each group of whales produces a specific number and type of these *discrete calls*, which together form its dialect. The group's dialect is apparently learned by each individual, probably by mimicking its mother as a calf. Each pod of resident killer whales has a unique dialect that can be readily identified by the trained ear or sound analyzer – some dialects are so distinctive that even an inexperienced listener can immediately discern the differences.

It may well be that dialects are used by the whales as acoustic indicators of group identity and membership, which might serve to preserve the integrity and cohesiveness of the social unit. Whatever their function for the whales, dialects provide us with insight into the social history of populations. Within the resident population, pods with related dialects belong to a *clan*. Each clan is most likely a continuous lineage that has descended from a common ancestral pod. As pods grew in size over time, they gradually split into new pods, and their common dialect drifted apart. This process may have repeated itself several times within each lineage, resulting in the complex systems of pod dialects we see today. Pods with very similar dialects probably split in the recent past, while others with fewer similarities likely have more distant relationships. Different clans have no dialect features in common and probably have very ancient links.

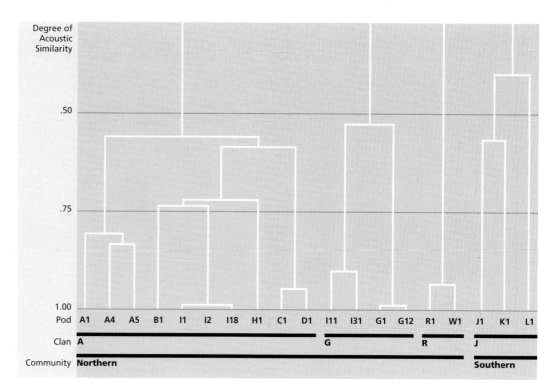

Vocal dialects of resident killer whale pods provide information on how communities have evolved in the past. This diagram shows all 19 resident pods organized according to the degree of similarity in their repertoires of calls. Pods with almost identical dialects are linked with a high index of acoustic similarity, and they in turn are linked to others with less acoustic similarity. Pods that have related dialects belong to the same clan. The four resident clans thus have no acoustic similarity and are not linked together. The degree of dialect similarity between pods probably indicates how closely they are related. The "family tree" shown for each clan reflects its historical genealogy.

*Newborn killer whales nurse for at least a year. The minimum interval between calves is three years, although, for some females, a decade or more may pass between successful calves.*

(Communication and echolocation of residents are also described in the sidebar on p. 75.)

Dialects of transients are, predictably, very different from those of residents. Transient dialects are made up of a relatively small repertoire of 4 to 6 different discrete calls, compared to the repertoires of 7 to 17 calls that form resident dialects. No calls are shared by the two types of killer whales. Most significantly, all transient groups recorded to date have the same basic dialect. This homogeneity of calls is probably a reflection of the fluid social system of transients. Because transient group membership frequently changes, there is little opportunity for group-specific sounds to develop within a lineage. The transient dialect is so widespread and distinctive, it has become one of the criteria we use to assign newly identified whales to the transient community.

Killer whales belonging to the offshore population are highly vocal, and preliminary analysis suggests that they produce calls unlike any resident or transient. There is even some evidence of group-specific dialects within this community, but much more research is needed to describe them in detail.

## Population Parameters

Detailed documentation of the resident killer whale population over the past twenty years has provided important information on the life history of the species. Although most of the statistics below were obtained from this population, they are probably representative of transients, offshores, and other populations as well.

The timing of many events in a killer whale's life is not unlike that of humans. In most cases, females give birth for the first time at 14 or 15 years, which is also near the age of reproductive maturity in human females. The youngest female we have seen with a calf was 11 years old. Studies of breeding in aquaria indicate that the gestation period is 16 to 17 months. Single young are usually born, although we have recorded one set of twins. Calves are about 2.5 metres long at birth and weigh 200 kilograms. For reasons that are not known, the mortality rate of calves is quite high – over 40% of resident calves die in their first year. A typical female produces 4 to 6 surviving offspring over a 25-year period, then stops breeding. Post-reproductive females may live for an additional 20 or more years after giving birth for the last time. The average lifespan of females appears to be about 50 years. However, from the number and age of offspring and descendants of some old females, we estimate that some may reach 80 years of age.

Male killer whales begin maturing at 12 to 14 years of age. Over the next few years, they grow very quickly and attain physical maturity at about 20 years. Most males probably reach a length of 8 to 9 metres, while females average about 7 metres. Although we cannot estimate the age of males from the number of their offspring, we know that some live to be at least 40 years old. Male longevity, however, seems to be less than that of females, averaging about 29 years.

# Resident Killer Whale Societies

Due to the abundance and predictability of resident killer whales in protected coastal waters, and as a result of their unusually stable social system, we have been able to collect considerably more information about this population than for transient and offshore whales. Annual field studies over the past twenty years have enabled us to assemble detailed genealogical histories for each of the 305 whales currently in the population. In this section and the next, we describe these resident societies and present a catalogue containing individual photographs and names for every whale in the population.

The social lives of resident killer whales are without doubt as rich and complex as those of the most advanced land mammals. The bonds among females and their offspring are extremely strong and persist throughout the whale's life. It is this long-term relationship between mother and young that is the most significant feature of resident societies, and it accounts for the kinds of social structures that we see in the population. Resident killer whales live in groups that are organized along lines of maternal relatedness. Each whale belongs to a matrilineal genealogy, that is, a family tree showing an individual's ancestry through its mother and her relatives.

In this study, relationships among individual whales were determined from their associations with each other while travelling. However, this technique only allows us to identify the maternal lineage, as paternity is unknown. Males are unlikely to mate with females in their pod and thus fathers probably travel in other social groups than their offspring. Travelling associations were determined by direct field observations as well as through analysis of photographs. The latter method involved two techniques. The first consisted of selecting representative pictures with several whales and determining the level of association by the distance between the whales. The second photographic technique involved the use of over 50,000 photos collected from 1973 to 1986. A computer program was designed to evaluate the number of times individuals appeared together, which resulted in an "index of association." The results of each kind of analysis were largely the same.

All ages and both sexes of whales tend to spend the greatest proportion of their time travelling with their mothers. For the first year of life, a nursing calf seldom strays far from its mother's side. Then, as a juvenile, it will spend some time interacting with siblings and whales in other groups, but still swims most frequently close to its mother. As the whale grows older, the association weakens somewhat, especially for female offspring once they give birth to their own young. However, the tendency continues well into adulthood, and we have concluded that a whale will stay primarily in the same social group as its mother as long as she is alive.

As our study is only twenty years old, and whales may live sixty or more years, it has taken some extrapolation from our observations to arrive at such a conclusion. First, numerous offspring that were born early in the study have matured during the course of our observations. Several of these are females and now have their own calves. In all cases, these whales have continued to travel closely with their mothers. Assuming that the adult female accompanying each medium- and large-sized juvenile observed at the beginning of the study was the mother, then these animals have continued to travel with their mothers as adults. No changes in travelling companions have been observed during the past two decades. Thus, extending this logic, we conclude that resident whales travel primarily with their mothers throughout their lives.

It was not without some surprise that we came to the realization that resident society is so strongly matrilineal. When the study began, many speculated that killer whale pods were the primary breeding units. The mature bulls in the group were thought to be the "harem masters," and they mated with the pod's cows. The calves and juveniles were therefore their offspring. This was not an unreasonable assumption, however, as many social carnivores live in groups with this kind of social system. But numerous other mammals, including some of the most socially advanced species, such as primates, live in multi-generation, matrilineal societies. However, in most of these matrilineal species, offspring, usually just males, disperse from the group upon reaching maturity and join other groups for breeding. This is probably also the case for certain other species of toothed cetaceans, such as bottlenose dolphins and sperm whales, which appear to live in matrilineal groups for at least part of their lives. Dispersal is thought to be primarily a mechanism by which the animals prevent excessive inbreeding. We are not certain how resident killer whales avoid the problem of inbreeding, but we believe that males will mate with unrelated cows when different groups are temporarily travelling together.

Resident societies can be organized into a series of social units according to maternal genealogy. The bonds within these units get progressively weaker, and the relatedness of the whales probably diminishes as one goes from the smallest social unit, the *matrilineal group*, through *subpod, pod, clan,* and finally to the largest, the *community*. The general features of each of these social levels is described below:

**Matrilineal group.** The matrilineal group is the basic social unit of resident killer whales. It is comprised of a mother and her offspring. If the female offspring are mature and have their own young, these are also part of the same matrilineal group. Many resident matrilineal groups consist of three generations, and some, we believe, contain four (a great-grandmother and her descendants). Individuals in a matrilineal group virtually always travel together and they are often seen right next to each other, especially when the whales are resting. Matrilineal groups are usually comprised of three to four individuals, but may contain up to nine whales.

**Subpod.** A subpod is a social unit containing one or more matrilineal groups that typically travel together at all times. Only rarely have we observed a subpod to fragment for more than a day or two. The females in matrilineal groups within a subpod are likely to be closely related, such as mothers, sisters, daughters, or cousins. We have never seen an individual move permanently from one subpod to another. Thus, individuals seem to remain in the subpod throughout their lives. Subpods share a common vocal dialect, although some can be differentiated by subtle differences in their calls. Subpods are comprised of one to eleven matrilineal groups, although most contain two.

**Pod.** A pod is a larger social unit consisting of subpods that tend to travel preferentially with one another. It is not uncommon for a subpod to leave the main pod for periods of weeks or months. The placement of subpods (especially those that separate for extended periods of time) into their appropriate pod must be determined from long-term associations or from pod dialects. Each pod can be distinguished acoustically. Pods consist of between one and five subpods, and most contain ten to twenty whales.

**Clan.** The clan is the next level of social structure above the pod. It is comprised of pods that have similar vocal dialects and thus are considered to be related to one another. All pods within a clan have most likely descended from a common ancestral pod through a process of growth and fragmentation along matrilines. Thus, the related dialects of clan members seem to be a vocal reflection of the common matrilineal heritage of the pods. Those pods with very similar dialects are probably more closely related, and have split more recently, than those with distinctive features in their dialects. We have no idea how different clans may be related as they have no dialect features in common. Perhaps each clan represents a separate lineage that, through an ancestral founding pod, independently colonized this section of the coast.

It is interesting that we often see little indication of the relatedness of pods, as determined from dialects, in their travel associations. Some pods will frequently swim with distantly related groups in preference to their close acoustical relatives. Pods choose different travel associates at different times, based probably on social factors such as age and sex composition. Dialects are very stable over time, however, and appear to better indicate pod genealogies than do associations.

**Community.** The top level of social structure is the community, which is made up of pods that have been observed together at least once during the study. Pods from one community have never been seen to travel with those from another, although their ranges partly overlap (see map, p. 17). There are two resident communities in coastal waters of British Columbia and Washington State, the *northern* and the *southern* communities. The northern community ranges through BC coastal waters from roughly the midpoint of Vancouver Island north to southeast Alaska, as well as the Queen Charlotte Islands. The range of the southern community includes waters off the southern half of Vancouver Island and Puget Sound. At last count (1993), the northern community was composed of 16 pods with a total of 209 whales, and the southern had 3 pods with 96 whales. The northern community contains 3 clans and the southern community a single clan.

It is important to note that the social structure of residents is not static. The process of change is a slow one, to be sure, but it is constantly under way nonetheless. The resident population has grown at a rate of 2-3% per year during our study, and mathematical models tell us that it has probably done so since the 1960s. The northern community, for example, is about one-third larger today than it was in 1973. As pods grow in size, they are more likely to split into subpods, which may themselves become pods in time. New pods may take decades to establish. Some pods (e.g., pod A1) contain subpods that spent the majority of their time together in the 1970s, but gradually spent more and more time apart through the 1980s, and now are seen separately more often than together. They still tend to associate more with one another than with different pods, however, and so we still consider them to be a single pod. The death of an old, post-reproductive cow – the matriarch of the group – can destabilize a subpod or pod and trigger the beginning of the splitting process. Not all pods grow and form new pods, however. If a pod has few or no reproductive females, its size may only just be maintained or it may decline. For example, the northern community pod W1 will eventually disappear because its only female is post-reproductive.

There are still a number of important gaps in our under-

*Large aggregations of resident killer whales are common during the summer months, when salmon are migrating and concentrated in coastal channels. Here, several resident pods are resting together.*

mines group size and stability? Most likely the ultimate factor is ecological. Group living provides an advantage to each whale by improving its success in locating and capturing prey – in this case, mostly salmon. But why are some pods several times the size of others, and why do some pods often fragment into subpods while others rarely or never do so? These kinds of variations are probably determined by the age and sex composition of the group, which in turn influences social dynamics. The numbers of matriarchs, mature males, or young whales in the pod may all play some role in determining the social patterns of the pod. For example, we have noticed that subpods containing more than the average proportion of bulls are more independent in their travelling patterns than those with a balanced sex ratio. The details of the various forces shaping social structures may require decades of additional fieldwork to resolve.

How typical of killer whales around the world is the social organization of our resident population? It is only in the last few years that it has been possible to shed some light on this question. Since the mid-1980s, photo-identification studies have been undertaken in Alaska, and the social structure seen there is very familiar. In Prince William Sound, there is a community of ten resident, salmon-eating pods that are composed of matrilineal groups and subpods. There is also a separate community of mammal-hunting transient groups in the area. In Norway, colleagues have recently conducted similar research on a population of herring-eating killer whales, and resident-like social structures seem to be the rule. Killer whales that have been studied by photo-identification in the sub-Antarctic Crozet Islands and Argentina are primarily mammal-hunters and have a lifestyle and social structure more typical of transients. It appears that resident-type societies may only occur in areas where there is abundant and reliable food resources, such as salmon or herring, and where there is an advantage for whales to remain in the same group for life.

standing of resident societies. One of the most puzzling is that individuals never leave the group into which they are born. Whales almost certainly mate outside their pod, as mentioned above, to avoid inbreeding. But who do they choose to mate with, and who does the choosing, males or females? We occasionally observe mating in the field, but never with enough confidence to predict when a female will give birth or who the calf's father might be. It is possible that dialects – another very unusual feature of resident cultures – may have a role in the mating system. Perhaps whales choose mating partners who sound different from themselves and are thus not close relatives. Whales might favour mating partners in different clans, although this is not an option for the southern community, which consists of a single clan. Only through genetic studies, which are currently under way, will we solve the mysteries of paternity and mating systems in resident society.

Another question that we often ask about resident social organization is simple but difficult to answer: What deter-

# Watching Killer Whales

Watching killer whales in the wild in British Columbia and Washington State has developed into a popular recreational activity over the past decade. Nothing quite matches the thrill of witnessing a resident pod cutting through the waters of Johnstone Strait in pursuit of salmon, or seeing a transient group combing the kelp beds in their hunt for seals. Listening to a pod's strident underwater calls as the whales keep in touch in their own dialect enhances this fascinating experience. There are two principal ways to view killer whales in the wild – from land and from boats.

## Land-Based Whale Watching

The whales can be seen from land anywhere along the coast, but there are few sites that offer a good opportunity to see them with some certainty. At present, the most reliable and accessible site for public viewing from land is Lime Kiln State Whale Watch Park, located on the west side of San Juan Island, overlooking Haro Strait. This park was established in 1984 by the Washington State Parks and Recreation Commission for the purpose of watching killer whales. Southern resident pods can be seen almost every day during summer, often at close range.

Most of the range of the northern resident community is accessible only by boat. However, there are plans to develop a trail from Telegraph Cove east along the Vancouver Island shoreline in the near future, which will provide good opportunities for viewing whales in western Johnstone Strait. It is also hoped that a land-based whale-watching site will be developed near the Robson Bight (Michael Bigg) Ecological Reserve, which people could access by shuttle water-taxi. As interest in whale watching continues to grow, viewing from shore may be an excellent way to accommodate large numbers of people without adding to vessel congestion around the whales.

## Vessel-Based Whale Watching

Whale watching can be done from all types and sizes of vessels, both private and commercial. Many people choose to

1. The bull A5 and his mother A9 (deceased, 1990) are photo-identified as they cruise slowly in Johnstone Strait.

2. The conical, interlocking teeth of killer whales are well suited for a wide variety of prey, from small schooling fish to large whales.

take one of many tour boats that offer killer whale watching. There are a variety of day-long or half-day excursions operating through the summer months in Haro Strait and Johnstone Strait. Some commercial tour operators also offer longer trips by kayak or sailboat. Organized whale-watching excursions have crew who are knowledgeable about killer whale natural history and identification. Some people prefer to view whales from their own boat or one they have chartered. Sea kayaks are an economical option, and these can be easily rented and transported by car to good whale-watching areas. Sailboats and motor vessels are also popular. Whale watchers are urged to follow the guidelines set forth in "How to Behave Around Killer Whales" (p. 57) to minimize disturbance.

## Interpreting Whale Activities and Behaviours

Like all social mammals, killer whales exhibit a wide variety of behaviours as they go about their daily lives. Unlike their terrestrial counterparts, however, these marine mammals spend the majority of their time underwater and thus out of sight of vessel- or shore-based observers. For this reason, we must infer much of the whales' behaviour from relatively short glimpses at the surface and by eavesdropping with underwater hydrophones. Until such time as technology enables us to view wild whales as they swim underwater, the details of their subsurface behaviours are left to the observer's imagination.

The activities of resident killer whale groups fall into four rather broad categories: *foraging, travelling, resting,* and *socializing.* Although members of subpods or pods tend to coordinate their activities, these categories are not entirely exclusive. Some whales in a group may be foraging, for example, while others nearby are socializing or resting. Within specific activity states, the whales tend to exhibit characteristic surface behaviours, but again these are not exclusive. Some behaviours, such as tail slapping, may be observed during all four activity categories. In the following section, we describe each activity state, and the kinds of group and individual behaviours that one typically sees. It should be noted that our knowledge of whale activities is based mostly on observations in daylight hours during the months of May through November. We believe that whales behave similarly during the hours of darkness, but their activities during winter are very poorly understood.

**Foraging.** The most common activity of resident killer whales is foraging. This activity includes all occasions where the whales are feeding or appear to be searching for food. When foraging, members of pods spread out, often over areas of several square kilometres, with individuals or small subgroups diving and surfacing independently while swimming generally in the same direction. The whales often move forward in a loosely organized broad front, as if they are sweeping an area for fish. In narrow passages, such as Johnstone Strait, some individuals can often be found close to the shore on each side of the Strait, while others, especially mature males, swim out in the channel. Foraging whales typically make two or three short, shallow dives, followed by a longer dive of one to three minutes. The whales produce underwater vocalizations frequently during foraging, presumably to keep group members in touch with one another.

The amount of time killer whale groups engage in foraging can vary widely. In areas or at times of the year when salmon are relatively scarce, the whales may spend entire days foraging. During the peak of salmon abundance in Johnstone or Haro straits, however, bouts of foraging may only last two or three hours before the whales begin a different activity. During the summer, resident killer whales in Johnstone Strait spend about 65% of their time foraging. Visual signs of successful fish capture are often subtle, such as a whale briefly changing direction or making a slight lunge at the surface. Sometimes, however, an individual makes a spectacular dash through the water, culminating in an explosion of spray as it captures its prey. Usually the only evidence of a kill is a few scales or bits of flesh drifting in the water. Whenever possible, we collect such remains and use them to identify the species involved. Almost all resident kills we have documented were of salmon, and included all six species found on the coast.

**Travelling.** A group of whales is considered to be travelling when it is swimming consistently in one direction at a moderate to fast pace, usually in a relatively tight formation, and there is no sign of feeding. Travelling whales tend to move at speeds of 5 knots or more, compared to the more leisurely pace of 2-3 knots exhibited during foraging. It is not uncommon for a rapidly travelling group to surface and dive in unison, or for individuals to clear the water's surface as they come up to breathe. Travelling seems to be simply a means of transiting an area, perhaps to move from one good feeding spot to another. In western Johnstone Strait, travelling activity is fairly uncommon, apparently because the foraging routine of the whales in the area is confined to a small area. Travelling is more often observed among southern resident whales than northern residents. At most times, travelling whales are highly vocal, but occasionally a group will travel in silence.

**Resting.** Following a bout of foraging, members of killer whale pods and subpods often get together and begin resting. This activity, the whales' version of sleep, is quite distinctive and easily recognizable at the surface. The whales typically group tightly together abreast, forming a line of animals that dives and surfaces as a cohesive unit. The arrangement of individuals in a resting line is usually determined by genealogy. Offspring tend to cluster around their mother, often appearing to be in physical contact, and surface for air in a characteristic sequence. If many whales are present, they group according to the appropriate subpod or pod. At such times, there may be several resting lines in close proximity.

When resting, whales slow down and usually become very quiet underwater. Dives and surfacings become highly regular; the group has several short, shallow surfacings over a period of 2-3 minutes, then dives for 3-5 minutes. Forward progression of the group continues, albeit at a slow pace of 1-2 knots or less. Episodes of resting may last from less than an hour to more than 7 hours, with an average duration of about 2 hours. During the summer months, when most behavioural data have been recorded, resident whales spend about 13% of their time resting.

**Socializing.** The fourth activity category of residents, socializing, includes a great variety of physical interactions and displays among individuals. An entire group of whales can be simultaneously involved in socializing, or only a few individuals may socialize while others forage or rest. Behaviours seen during socializing episodes include sexual interactions, often among all-male subgroups, and various aerial displays such as breaching, spyhopping, tail slapping, and flipper slapping. Whales often chase one another, or roll and thrash together at the surface. Individuals may also interact with inanimate objects such as floating kelp, and will occasionally surf in the wake of passing boats. Socializing behaviours are often most common and vigorous among juvenile whales, and seem to represent a form of play.

Periods of socializing activity last about two hours on average and account for approximately 15% of the whale's time during the summer months. Socializing whales often group together and dive for long periods, not unlike the patterns seen during resting activity. However, in addition to the increased levels of excitement, socializing whales tend to be far more vocal than resting whales. The types of vocalizations produced during socializing tend to differ quite markedly from those of foraging or travelling whales. Unlike the repetitive stereotyped calls used in the latter contexts, socializing whales employ a wide range of highly variable squeaks, squawks, and whistles. Although the functions of these unusual signals are not known, they probably serve an important social role when used in conjunction with physical and visual displays during socializing.

One particularly unusual form of socializing activity is beach rubbing. This behaviour takes place only among northern resident whales – the southern residents have never been seen to rub on any beach, nor have transient killer whales. Although several beaches in the range of the northern residents are known to serve as occasional rubbing sites, the behaviour is most common and regular at a series of small beaches within the Robson Bight (Michael Bigg) Ecological Reserve in Johnstone Strait. The whales may visit these beaches several times in a 24-hour period, where they rub their bodies on the small, smooth pebbles for up to an hour or more. Most evidence points to beach rubbing being a social or "recreational" behaviour, although it may also have some practical application, such as being a way of removing external parasites. Rubbing is usually exhibited in the context of other socializing behaviours or resting, and probably represents a behavioural tradition that has developed over generations within the northern resident community, but not among the southern residents. If some form of external parasite is involved, presumably this is not a problem in the southern community.

Although southern resident whales do not appear to rub, they have social traditions that differ somewhat from northern residents. When socializing, for example, southern residents appear to exhibit more vigorous and frequent aerial displays, such as breaches, than do northern residents. Also, when southern resident pods meet after separation of a day or two, they often engage in a distinctive behaviour referred to as a "greeting ceremony." As two pods approach each other, they form two lines and stop at the surface when 10 to 50 metres apart. After less than a minute, the two groups then submerge and a great deal of social excitement and vocal activity ensues as they swim and mill together in tight subgroups. This form of display has occasionally been seen among the northern residents, but it is far more common among the southern whales.

### Does Watching Whales Bother Them?

Many whale enthusiasts are concerned about the potential disturbance to killer whales from whale-watching vessels. This concern is also shared by whale researchers, many of whom have tried to objectively assess the impacts of vessels. Unfortunately, we do not yet have enough clear evidence to determine whether whale-watching boats and other types of marine traffic are detrimental to the well-being of the whales.

*opposite page: Killer whales occasionally play with kelp by draping it over their dorsal fin or lifting it in the air with their tail flukes.*

1. *A frisky juvenile surfs in the wake of a research boat. Resident whales have been seen riding the wake of all types of vessels, from small skiffs to the largest cruise ships.*

2. *Spyhopping is a behaviour where a whale raises its head out of the water, presumably for a look above the surface. Killer whales have good vision both above and below the water.*

*opposite page: A whale throws spray into the air as it raises its flukes after slapping the water's surface. Tail slapping is a behaviour that allows for both visual and acoustic communication, although it is not always clear what the whale is signalling. Whales may tail slap while socializing, after resting, or when disturbed.*

Disturbance to killer whales from boats can potentially come in many different forms, some of which are very difficult to measure. The sudden approach of a boat can startle a whale or cause short-term disruption of a pod's activities. Typically, the whales seem to recover quickly from such isolated incidents and do not reveal any lasting effect. However, if disruptive encounters take place repeatedly – and they do at certain times in some areas – it seems likely that there will be a cumulative, negative impact. If whales are followed by a number of boats, hour after hour or have to negotiate a fleet of vessels in their path, this will probably lead to some form of stress.

Vessel traffic generates much underwater noise, which may affect the whales' ability to hear the communication sounds of distant companions or perhaps limits their ability to navigate and find food by echolocation.

If long-term effects of vessels exist, they have eluded detection by researchers. Resident killer whales have long frequented waterways that are busy with marine traffic, and they seem to have adapted to the underwater noise and commotion. Although survey effort has varied over the years, resident whales appear to use the core areas of Johnstone and Haro straits as much now as they did twenty years ago, despite steady increases in the amount of whale-oriented boat activity. However, we must be vigilant and continue to closely monitor whale occurrence and behaviour in order to detect any signs of possible disturbance. At the same time, it is important that we act in a cautious manner when viewing or studying whales, and that we manage our activities conservatively. Research has confirmed that northern residents are particularly sensitive to human activities at their traditional rubbing beaches in the Robson Bight (Michael Bigg) Ecological Reserve in Johnstone Strait, and for this reason the area is off-limits to whale watchers and researchers without a special permit (see sidebar, p. 57).

For most people interested in viewing killer whales in the wild, we recommend that they choose one of the established commercial tour excursions (see sidebar, p. 53). The operators of these vessels are generally very familiar with the whales and their habits, and are careful not to approach them in a manner that might cause disturbance. Most also carry underwater hydrophones for listening in on the whales' vocal exchanges. Watching whales in the coastal waters of British Columbia and Washington is a wonderful experience, yet it is a privilege that we should not abuse. Done properly, future generations will also be able to witness these remarkable animals in their natural habitat.

*Resident whales exhibit a variety of behaviours while undertaking their daily activities. Beach rubbing (left) is a common behaviour of northern residents, especially at certain pebble beaches in the Robson Bight (Michael Bigg) Ecological Reserve, but it is not observed among southern residents. Speed swimming (upper right) is often seen when whales are travelling quickly from one feeding location to another. Most of the time, however, whales swim at a more sedate pace while foraging (lower right).*

When resting, members of pods or subpods group closely together and cruise slowly and quietly. The female A28 rests with her two probable uncles, A26 and A5 (upper left). A group of northern residents lazes at the surface near the Robson Bight (Michael Bigg) Ecological Reserve in Johnstone Strait (right). As whales begin "waking up" from a period of resting, they often exhibit aerial behaviours such as flipper slapping, where an individual raises its pectoral flipper above the surface and strikes it forcefully on the water (lower left). Flipper slaps make a loud sound that can carry for up to a kilometre underwater. As with other aerial displays, the function of this behaviour is not certain.

*While travelling at high speed, killer whales often begin exhaling before surfacing (left). When swimming at regular speeds, however, they exhale at the surface, creating the plume of fine mist typical of a blow (right). A breach (lower right) occurs when a whale leaps out of the water, exposing two-thirds or more of its body. Breaches may take place at any time when a group is active and are exhibited by all age classes. The function of breaches is not clear, but it probably varies with each situation.*

# Catalogue of Resident Killer Whales

What follows is an overview of the social composition of the resident killer whales of the northern and southern communities, and of the methods used to identify the groups in the field. An identification photograph of each whale is presented, along with the individual's known or estimated year of birth, and its sex, again where known. The whales are arranged according to their position in their matrilineal group, subpod, pod, clan, and community. First, however, it is important to have some background on how whales and the various levels of social structure are named, as well as on the technique of individual identification.

## The Naming System

We developed our naming system during the course of our research. The plan was to assign the same letter to each whale within a pod and then to give each individual whale a number. The following is an historical account of the identification of the first pod, which will explain some of the system's idiosyncracies.

The first whale recognized was called A1, and because she was so well marked her pod was called A1 pod. As chance would have it, during our first encounters with her pod, we did not realize that the pod actually consisted of three pods which just happened to be travelling together, and we erroneously considered all of the whales to be members of her pod. When we discovered our error, it was too late to change the names of the whales in the other two pods. We simply split A1's group into three pods and called each new pod after its most distinctive member. The resulting pods were A1, A4, and A5. Each whale in the three pods has the prefix A in its name and is numbered according to the order in which it was identified.

Similar situations arose several times in naming other pods. An important consequence of this naming system is that no significance with respect to genealogy or travel patterns should be given to the fact that pods have the same letter designation. For example, I11 and I31 pods belong to a different clan than I1, I2, or I18 pods, and are probably only distantly related. These pods all share the letter "I" simply because they happened to

*Differences in the appearance of the dorsal fin and saddle patch are used to recognize individuals. An identification photo of the female J4 is shown here, along with the features that make her distinctive.*

nick

dorsal fin

indentation

pigmentation detail

saddle patch

scar

*The first resident killer whale to be identified from markings on the dorsal fin was the old cow, A1, who died in 1974. Known as "Stubbs," this whale had sustained major damage to her dorsal fin, probably from a collision with a ship's propellor (see sidebar, p. 83).*
*Although A1 was easy to identify visually, the majority of whales have less distinct markings, and a good photograph or close examination with binoculars is needed for a positive identification.*

be together when first photo-identified. Also, some pods were named after whales that have since died.

Recently, we have modified our naming system to reflect the matrilineal structure of resident society. Subpods are named after the senior cow in the group, who may be an old, post-reproductive grandmother or a breeding female. Upon her death, the subpod is renamed after the next oldest reproductive female in the group. If there is no breeding female in the subpod, its name remains unchanged until a female starts reproducing or the subpod dies out. If a subpod splits, each new subpod is named after its oldest productive female. In the future, pods will be named after the senior matriarch in the group. Clans are named according to the first alphabetical designation of a member pod, hence the A, G, R, and J clans.

## How Whales Are Identified

As explained earlier, whales are identified individually from unique markings on their dorsal fin and the grey saddle patch at the base of the fin. Other features can also be used, such as the eye patch, but these are not as visible to the surface observer. The markings on the dorsal fin and saddle patch are documented by a high-quality black-and-white photograph, normally of the left side of the whale. The two sides often vary slightly in appearance, but, on occasion, one side is completely different. We arbitrarily chose the left side to simplify and standardize the system.

The unique characteristics of the dorsal fin are its shape, size, and scars. The scars are the result of injuries and are seen as gouges, nicks, and indentations, most of which are located along the rear edge of the fin. These injuries are permanent markings. The saddle patch, particularly its upper half, often has a unique shape. The shape does not change and its scarring and blemishes are frequently permanent. The location of the saddle patch relative to the ridge of the back and the detail of the edge of the pigmentation is also important.

We developed this recognition process over approximately ten years, and we can now distinguish many individuals on sight. However, we still rely mainly on photographs for identification, especially for whales with indistinct markings. The ability to recognize individuals develops with experience and can be classified according to three stages:

**Easy.** The easiest whales to recognize are those with major injuries to their dorsal fin. Such injuries consist of substantial tissue loss (e.g., I1, p. 63), the splitting and curling of the tip of the fin (e.g., C9, p. 58; G11, p. 70), tears (e.g., C10, p. 59), or bends (e.g., I3, p. 63; I5, p. 64). Spotting these features still requires observers to spend time looking at each whale to see the range of possible fin appearances. Once recognized, a well-marked whale can be readily distinguished. Most people will be content to reach this level.

**Difficult.** The majority of whales can only be identified by the examination of small injuries (e.g., G3, p. 68; K7, p. 86), or an unusually shaped saddle patch (e.g., A42, p. 54; G6, p. 68). Sometimes there are fairly noticeable scars on the saddle patch (e.g., A23, p. 55) or small indentations on the leading edge of the fin (e.g., J5, p. 85). Close examination of whales using binoculars or good photographs is required to identify these animals.

**Challenging.** The most difficult group to identify consists of those whales with no obvious distinguishing marks. The subtle features of dorsal fin and saddle patch shape are used, and a very good photograph is usually needed. Most small juveniles fit into this category. Fortunately, resident whales travel in established pods and some individuals can be recognized by identifying their companions. This is especially useful for juveniles, which travel very closely with their mothers. Their identities can be tentatively determined from these associations, then confirmed from photographs.

## Catalogue Organization

Identification photographs of individual whales are arranged by known or assumed genealogical relationships. Typically, the oldest whale – the matriarch – in the matrilineal group is placed at the top of the page, and her offspring are posi-tioned below her in order of increasing age from left to right. Below these, third- and fourth-generation offspring, when present, are arranged in the same manner. The catalogue includes photographs of all whales known to be alive in 1993, as well as several individuals that were alive in 1992 but missing in 1993 (if these whales are still missing in 1994, they will be considered dead). Also shown on each catalogue page is a schematic family tree for the matrilineal group(s), which includes whales that died during the study.

To assist in whale identification, we have prepared photographs in three size categories that reflect the body size of individuals:

**Calves and small juveniles** (height of photograph = 3.5 cm). This category includes young whales one to three years of age (born 1991-93). These small individuals are often difficult to photograph and are usually indistinctly marked.

**Older juveniles and adult females** (height of photograph = 4.5 cm). All whales born in 1990 or earlier, except adult males, are included in this category.

**Adult males** (height of photograph = 6.5 cm). The dorsal fin of males grows rapidly at the onset of puberty, usually around 13 to 15 years of age, and reaches a height of almost 2 metres at maturity. This category includes males whose fin is part way through this growth spurt or has reached full height.

Lines linking whales in matrilineal groups are of three types, which reflect different levels of certainty in genealogical assignment:

**Positive** (———). A solid line indicates relationships that we consider to be certain. Most whales born during the study (1973 or later) are linked in this way to their mothers.

**Probable** (··········). Whales that were born prior to the start of the study, but still juveniles when first seen, are linked with a

♀

♂

closely dotted line to the whale that is most likely to be their mother. Although the adult female with which it was closely associated was assumed to be its mother, the real mother may have died before the study began, and the juvenile may have formed a bond with another adult female.

**Possible** ( · · · · · ). A line of widely spaced dots is used to indicate the maternal relationship of a whale that was an adult when first seen. Although the association appears to be a strong bond and likely represents kinship, the actual lineage is the least certain. There is a real possibility that the actual mother may have died, or that the travel association with the presumed mother may have been formed on some basis other than genealogy.

As the study continues in the future, possible and probable linkages will gradually be replaced with positive relationships as old whales die and new whales are born. Of the 305 resident whales in the population, the mothers of 170 (56%) are positively known. Probable mothers have been identified for 67 whales (22%) and possible mothers for 25 (8%). Mothers of the remaining 43 whales (14%) were probably dead at the beginning of the study and thus are unknown.

**Sex and Year of Birth**

Above each whale's photograph in the catalogue we have indicated its sex, where known, and its estimated or actual year of birth. The sex of mature whales (over about 15 years old) is easy to determine because of the much larger dorsal fin of males relative to that of females. Establishing the gender of juveniles and calves, however, can be quite difficult. If a small whale happens to roll upside down at the surface, and if we are fortunate enough to get a clear view or photograph of its underside, its sex can be determined from distinctive pigmentation patterns in the genital area and from the presence of mammary slits in females. We know the gender of many juveniles and calves belonging to common pods because such opportunities have arisen. However, most young whales in less frequently seen pods are of uncertain gender and may remain so until they mature. We can occasionally obtain hints of gender, however, as both young and old males often form temporary "male play groups," and we have noted in the catalogue those whales that we suspect are male.

The year of birth given for whales varies widely in precision. For individuals born during the study (1973 and onwards), ages can be considered correct unless noted. We should point out, however, that since most whales are born during the late fall to spring period when little fieldwork is done, we are usually unsure whether a calf was born early in the new year or late in the previous year. To simplify our analysis, we have standardized all winter births to 1 January, except for the few cases where we know a whale was born late in the previous year.

For whales born prior to the beginning of the study, we have had to use various methods to estimate the year of birth. Those individuals that were immature, but not calves of the year when first identified, were aged by their relative size. Juveniles that were older when first seen were aged in reference to the year that they became sexually mature. These birth dates can be considered accurate to within ±2 years. Whales that were mature when identified were aged by indirect methods. For females, year of birth was estimated from the age of their offspring and the average age at which females cease reproduction (around 40 years). These estimates have potential inaccuracies of as much as ±12 years. For mature males without living mothers, it was not possible to estimate the year of birth. Instead, their ages are given as the latest year the whale could have been born (for more details on age estimation, see papers by Bigg et al. 1990 and Olesiuk et al. 1990, listed in the bibliography).

**Northern Resident Community**

The northern resident community is comprised of three clans – A, G, and R – with a total of 16 pods. In 1993, the population was made up of 200 whales, plus 9 individuals that were missing and may be dead. The community has grown by over 50% from an estimated size of 132 whales in 1975.

As mentioned previously, the range of the northern community includes coastal waters from approximately the mid-point of Vancouver Island north to southeast Alaska. Members of the community are most commonly seen during the months of June through October in the area of western Johnstone Strait and Queen Charlotte Strait, off northeastern Vancouver Island. It is in this region that salmon funnel into narrow channels on their way to spawning rivers, and the whales congregate here to intercept them. Whale researchers also tend to congregate in Johnstone Strait during summer, and, as a result, we know little of the whereabouts of whales outside of this area and season. Even during the peak of whale activity in Johnstone Strait in the summer, it is unusual to have more than 50, and rare to have more than 100, whales present on any given day. In the winter, northern residents turn up in Johnstone Strait periodically, but only in small numbers. Thus, the majority of northern residents are typically located in other parts of their range throughout the year.

We have observed or received photos of northern residents at many different locations in their range, but in no area are they found as predictably as in Johnstone Strait. Sightings have been made throughout the narrow inside passages of the central and northern BC coast, out on the fishing banks off the west coast of Vancouver Island, in the middle of Hecate Strait, and recently in the Queen Charlotte Islands. The range of northern residents includes many thousands of kilometres of inlets, channels, passes, and straits, much of it very remote. Perhaps it is not surprising that we know so little about the year-round distribution patterns of these whales.

Members of each of the three northern resident clans have been observed in most parts of the community range, indicating that there is no clan territoriality. Indeed, all 16 northern resident pods have been observed to travel together at least once, and most on repeated occasions. However, some pods appear to prefer certain portions of the range over others. For example, A1 pod (or one or more of its subpods) has been recorded in the western Johnstone Strait region on 1,119 occasions over the past 20 years, but its fellow A-clan member, I18 pod, has been sighted only 23 times in that area. Only with increased study effort in remote parts of the range will we have a clearer pic-

*Male and female killer whales can be distinguished by variations in the appearance of the pigmentation in the genital area. Females (upper photo, p. 44) have dark spots marking the two mammary slits, located on either side of the genital slit, which also usually has a dark marking. The genital area is surrounded by a roughly circular or oval white patch. Males (lower photo, p. 44) have a more pronounced dark spot at the genital slit, lack mammary slits, and have a more elongated white patch surrounding the genital slit. Note the long pectoral flippers of the adult male which, together with the large dorsal fin and downward curled tail flukes, are sexual characteristics typical of mature bulls.*

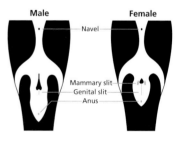

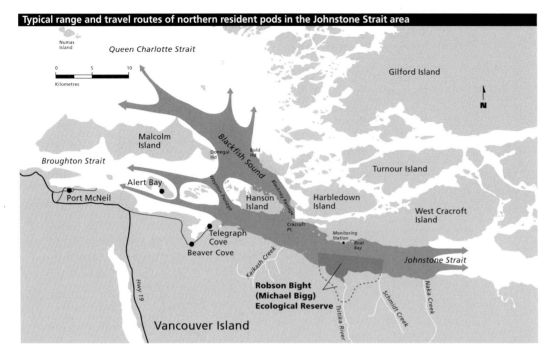

**Typical range and travel routes of northern resident pods in the Johnstone Strait area**

Numas Island

Queen Charlotte Strait

Gilford Island

Kilometres

0   5   10

N

Malcolm Island

Donegal Hd

Blackfish Sound

Bold Hd

Broughton Strait

Alert Bay

Voynton Passage

Turnour Island

Port McNeil

Hanson Island

Harbledown Island

Blackney Passage

West Cracroft Island

Cracroft Pt.

Telegraph Cove

Monitoring Station

Beaver Cove

Boat Bay

Johnstone Strait

Kaikash Creek

Hwy 19

Robson Bight (Michael Bigg) Ecological Reserve

Schmidt Creek

Naka Creek

Tsitika River

Vancouver Island

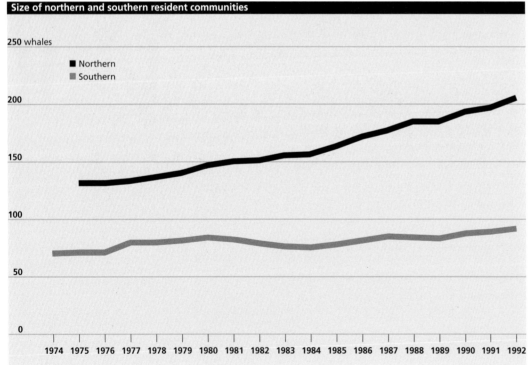

**Size of northern and southern resident communities**

250 whales

■ Northern
■ Southern

200

150

100

50

0

1974 1975 1976 1977 1978 1979 1980 1981 1982 1983 1984 1985 1986 1987 1988 1989 1990 1991 1992

ture of distribution patterns at the subpod, pod, or clan level.

The following is a summary of the composition of the northern resident clans. Further details about pods and sub-pods accompany their identification photographs.

**A-Clan.** The A-clan is comprised of ten pods, A1, A4, A5, B1, C1, D1, H1, I1, I2, and I18, with a total of 116 whales. As with all clans, these pods have dialect similarities which suggest that they are part of a single lineage. Within the clan, certain pods are more closely related than others, as shown in the diagram of A-clan dialect similarity (p. 21). Pods A1, A4, and A5 are fairly closely related to one another, and C1 and D1 are also quite closely related. Pods I1, I2, and I18 share essentially the same dialect, although further study may reveal some group-specific features in their sounds.

The A-clan includes the best-known northern resident pods as well as the least-known. Pods A1, A4, A5, and C1 are the most common pods in the Johnstone Strait area, having each been observed many hundreds of times during our study. On the other hand, pods I1 and I18 have been sighted less than 30 times each.

**G-Clan.** The G-clan contains four pods, G1, G12, I11, and I31, with 67 whales in total. G-clan pods are sighted less frequently than most A-clan pods, but more often than R-clan pods. Pods G1 and G12 formerly were considered to be a single pod, but were split into two when it became clear that they spent a significant amount of time apart. The two are very difficult to separate acoustically, as are pods I11 and I31. Members of the G-clan are sighted off the west coast of Vancouver Island more often than other northern resident pods. Also, G1 and G12 pods tend to frequent the Johnstone Strait area most often in the late summer and fall.

**R-Clan.** The R-clan is the smallest clan, containing only 26 members in two pods, R1 and W1. The two have almost identical dialects, although they can be distinguished from subtle differences in call use. Although R-clan pods have been sighted as far south as Georgia Strait, there is some evidence that they frequent the northern portions of the community range more often than other community members.

## Southern Resident Community

The southern community is comprised of a single clan, J-clan, which is made up of three pods, J1, K1, and L1. The population totalled 96 in 1993, which is 35% higher than its size of 71 when first censused in 1974. Unlike most northern community pods, all three southern resident pods were cropped during 1967-73 in a live-capture fishery for aquaria. An estimated 47 southern residents, mostly immature whales, were taken during this period, and this may have hindered growth of the population when compared to northern residents. Pod L1, with 59 members, is by far the largest resident pod. Of the three pods, J1 and K1 tend to be more acoustically related to each other than either is to L1 pod. The southern resident pods are seen most regularly during the summer in the protected inshore waters of Georgia Strait and Puget Sound, especially in the vicinity of Haro Strait, west of San Juan Island, and off the southern tip of Vancouver Island. Southern residents, especially pods K1 and L1, frequently make excursions out of Juan de Fuca Strait to areas off the west coast of Vancouver Island, where they mingle with commercial trollers on the offshore banks to catch salmon headed for the Fraser River. In September and October, all three pods can often be found off the mouth of the Fraser River in Georgia Strait, intercepting salmon before they enter the river. During the winter, J1 is the most common pod sighted in inshore waters, while K1 and L1 apparently spend more time in offshore areas.

The range of the southern residents overlaps with that of the northern residents in the waters off both the west and east coasts of Vancouver Island. For example, both northern and southern residents have been observed in northern Georgia Strait near Campbell River and offshore of Bamfield on the west coast of Vancouver Island. It is possible that the whales sometimes mix when they are in these overlap areas, but they have never been seen to do so.

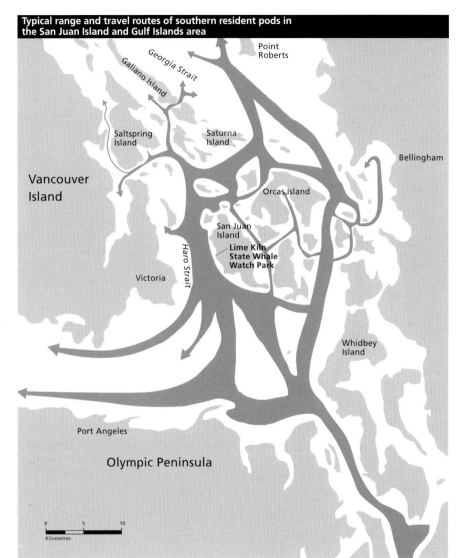

**Typical range and travel routes of southern resident pods in the San Juan Island and Gulf Islands area**

# A1 Pod
## A36 Subpod

**A36** ♀ 1947

**A20** ♂ 1953    *

*The A36 subpod will eventually die out unless the matriarch, A36, produces a surviving female offspring. A36 is nearing the end of her reproductive life, but was reported to have had a new calf late in 1993, which, hopefully, will survive and turn out to be a female. The first known matriarch of this subpod was the cow A1, known as "Stubbs" because of her lopped-off dorsal fin. A36's presumed brother, A20, was missing and probably dead in 1993.*

**A32** ♂ 1964

**A37** ♂ 1977

**A46** ♂ 1982

**Key**

| | |
|---|---|
| A1 ♀<br>1927–74 | Deceased killer whale with estimated or known birth date and date of death |
| * | missing in 1993 |
| c | live captured |

*Genealogical relationship:*

—————— Positive

················ Probable

· · · · · · Possible

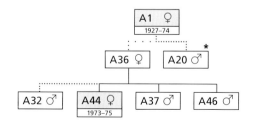

A-Clan

# A1 Pod
## A12 Subpod

**A12** ♀ 1941

A1 pod was the first group identified in this study. The pod's size has not changed much over the past 20 years – it had 13 members in 1973 and 15 in 1993 (assuming the male A20 is dead). However, its three subpods have steadlly been spending increasing time apart over the course of the study. In the 1970s, all three subpods were together in about two-thirds of encounters with A1 subpods. This dropped to one-third of encounters in the 1980s and one-fifth of encounters in the 1990s. Although the three subpods are now usually not seen together, each still travels more with other A1 subpods than any other northern resi-dent group.

**A31** ♂ 1958　　**A33** ♂ 1971　　**A34** ♀ 1975

**A55**　1990

*The cow A34 was reported to have had a new calf in November 1993, but no identification photos were taken.*

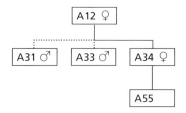

# A1 Pod
## A30 Subpod

**A30** ♀ 1947

**A6** ♂ 1964

**A38** ♂ 1970

**A39** ♂ 1975

**A50** ♀ 1984

**A54** ♀ 1989

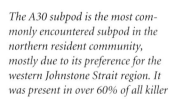

*The A30 subpod is the most commonly encountered subpod in the northern resident community, mostly due to its preference for the western Johnstone Strait region. It was present in over 60% of all killer whale encounters in this area. Until her death in 1989, the matriarch of the subpod was the well-known whale A2, or "Nicola."*

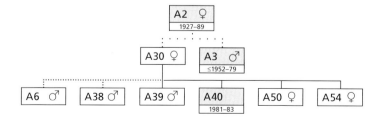

A2 ♀ 1927–89

A30 ♀ — A3 ♂ ≤1952–79

A6 ♂ | A38 ♂ | A39 ♂ | A40 1981–83 | A50 ♀ | A54 ♀

A-Clan

# A4 Pod
## A11 Subpod

A4 pod used to travel as one group with a single matriarch, A10, who died in 1983, along with her young calf A47, after being shot at the rubbing beaches in the Robson Bight (Michael Bigg) Ecological

Reserve. Starting in 1986, the pod began splitting into two subpods, A11 and A24. These two groups still spend the majority of their time together.

*The dialects of A11 and A24 subpods cannot yet be distinguished from each other. They are acoustically more closely related to A5 pod than to A1 pod.*

**A11** ♀ 1958

**A35** ♀ 1974

**A13** ♂ 1978

**A48** 1983

**A56** 1990

**A52** 1987

**A59** 1992

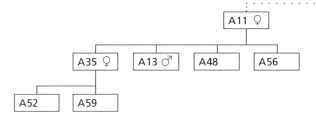

# A4 Pod
## A24 Subpod

**A24** ♀ 1967

**A45** ♀ 1983

**A53** ♀ 1988

\* **A58** 1992

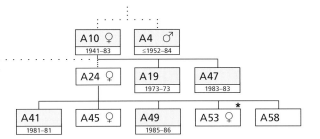

*The A24 subpod has had many young whales die. Two of A24's siblings died as calves, as did two of her own offspring. Another of A24's juveniles, A53, was missing in 1993.*

```
  A10 ♀     A4 ♂
 1941–83   ≤1952–84

      A24 ♀    A19      A47
              1973–73  1983–83

A41   A45 ♀   A49    A53 ♀   A58
1981–81      1985–86
                    *
```

## Whale-Watching Tours

The growing interest in whales has led to increasing numbers of people wanting to view them in the wild. Many people use their own boats or privately chartered vessels to see killer whales. Whale watching from one's own boat is unlikely to disturb the whales, if the guidelines given in 'How to Behave Around Killer Whales' (see sidebar, p. 57) are followed. However, as vessel congestion continues to increase in popular whale-watching areas such as Johnstone and Haro straits, joining an established whale-watching tour is a better option for both people and whales. Operators of these tours are generally careful not to disturb the whales, and their large vessels have the advantage of carrying many passengers, which is preferable to having a few whale watchers on many small boats. Most tours have onboard naturalists to explain killer whale biology, and good opportunities are provided for photographs.

There are now a variety of tour operators offering whale-watching excursions in both BC and Washington State. Most operate only during the months of June through September, when resident whales can be reliably found. Full- or half-day excursions are the most popular, although some companies offer longer trips of a week or more.

For information on whale-watching tours, contact:

*British Columbia*:

**Discover British Columbia**
**Parliament Buildings**
**Victoria, BC  V8V 1X4**
**1-800-663-6000 or (604) 387-1642**

**Tourism Association of Vancouver Island**
**(604) 382-3551**

*Washington State*:

**Washington Tourism**
**1-800-544-1800 or (206) 586-2102**

**Whale-Watching Line for San Juan Island**
**(206) 378-4710**

# A5 Pod
## A8 Subpod

**A8** ♀ 1953

**A28** ♀ 1974

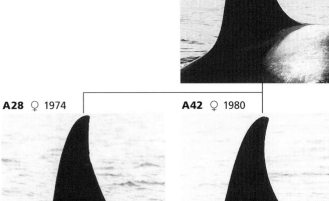

**A42** ♀ 1980

*A28 is one of the few females in the resident population that has been sexually mature for a number of years, but has never been seen with a calf.*

**A57** 1991

*A57 has a deformed rostrum ("nose"), causing its head to appear blunt. This kind of deformity has also been seen in a few other whales in the population.*

# A5 Pod
## A9 Subpod

**A5** ♂ 1957

**A26** ♂ 1971

A5 pod is one of the few northern resident pods that makes occasional forays into northern Georgia Strait. It was captured there twice, in 1968 and 1969, and a total of 12 whales were taken into captivity. Two of these are still alive in US oceanariums. The pod was only two members larger in 1993 than when first censused in 1973.

*The A9 subpod began spending time away from the rest of the pod in the mid-1980s, when A26 became mature. The matriarch, A9, died in late November 1990, and her body was recovered shortly thereafter from a beach in the Johnstone Strait area. Her stomach contained fish bones, representing 13 different species. Most common were salmon and lingcod, but also present were remains of various species of sole, flounder, greenlings, sculpins, and sablefish.*

*As the A9 subpod contains only males, it will die out in time. Following their mother's death, A5 and A26 spent considerable time apart from other groups. They now travel most consistently with the A8 subpod.*

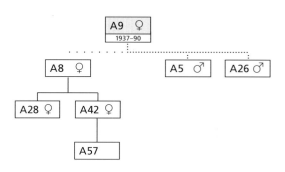

## A5 Pod
### A23 Subpod

**A23** ♀ 1947

*A23 is probably the mother of A16, also known as "Corky," who was captured at Pender Harbour in 1969 and presently lives at Sea World, in San Diego.*

**A27** ♂ 1971

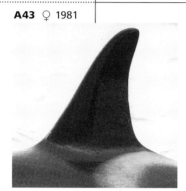

**A43** ♀ 1981

**A60** ♂ 1992

## A5 Pod
### A25 Subpod

**A25** ♀ 1971

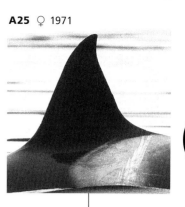

**A51** ♀ 1986

*The former matriarch of this sub-pod was A14, also known as "Saddle" because of her distinctively pigmented saddle patch. Her only surviving offspring is A25, called "Sharky" because of the distinctive shape of her dorsal fin. Two of A25's siblings were taken into captivity in 1969, and another, A15, vanished at the same time as their mother.*

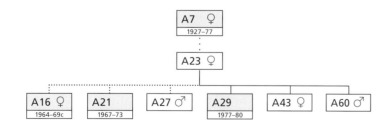

```
        A7 ♀
       1927–77
          ⋮
        A23 ♀

  A16 ♀   A21    A27 ♂   A29    A43 ♀   A60 ♂
1964–69c 1967–73       1977–80
```

*The whale A21 may be the juvenile struck by a ferry in an incident described on page 83.*

```
           A14 ♀
          1947–91

  A17    A18 ♀      A25 ♀   A15 ♂
1964–69c 1969–69c           1979–91

                    A51 ♀
```

# B1 Pod
## B7 Subpod

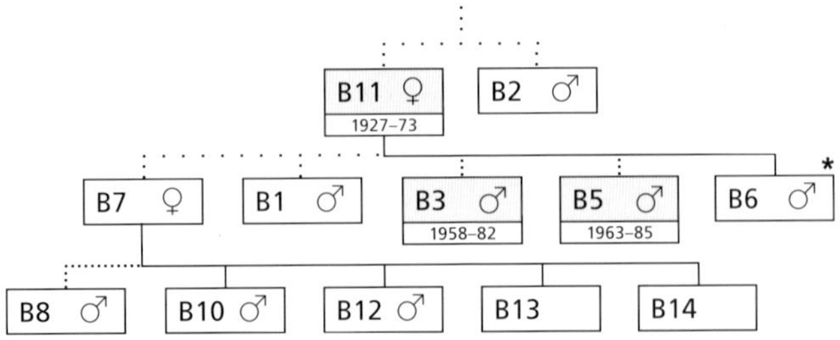

B11 ♀ 1927–73
B2 ♂

B7 ♀
B1 ♂
B3 ♂ 1958–82
B5 ♂ 1963–85
B6 ♂ *

B8 ♂
B10 ♂
B12 ♂
B13
B14

*The bull B1 has long been called "Hooker" because of the distinctive forward bend of his dorsal fin.*

B1 pod is rather unusual due to its high proportion of males. The pod also travels alone more than any other northern resident group – in about 25% of encounters with B1 pod, no other whales were present.

**B7** ♀ 1947

**B1** ♂ ≤1951

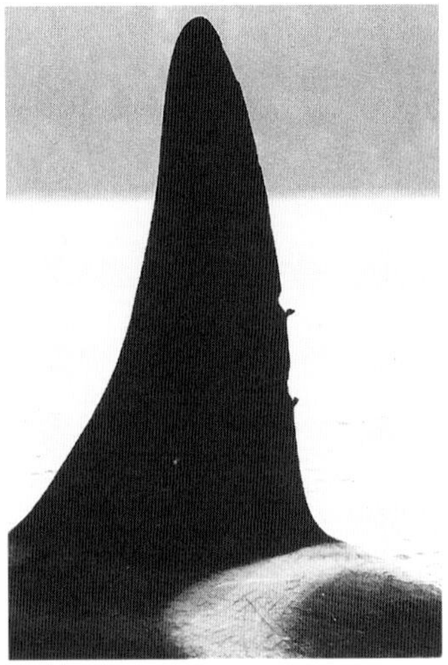

**B6** ♂ 1973

*

**B8** ♂ 1964

**B10** ♂ 1979

**B12** ♂ 1984

**B13** 1987

**B14** 1991

## How to Behave Around Killer Whales

When a boater encounters killer whales, either intentionally or by chance, the question immediately arises: How can I get the best view of them? More and more, people are also asking: How can I get a good view without disturbing the whales?

Killer whales tend to travel in a particular direction, usually at a speed of 2-4 knots, and are likely to continue to do so if undisturbed. The dive pattern of residents usually consists of a long dive of 3-4 minutes, followed by several short dives of about 15 seconds each. Transient whales tend to dive longer and to be more unpredictable than residents. A pod may travel in a tightly packed group for a while and then disperse into small groups over a wider area, usually to forage.

The following guidelines allow boaters to view whales in the least obtrusive way:

1 From a distance, determine the travel direction and diving sequence of the whales.
2 Approach whales from the side, not from the front or the rear. Approach and depart slowly, avoiding sudden changes in speed or direction. Do not "leapfrog." Avoid disturbing groups of resting whales.
3 Maintain low speeds and constant direction if travelling parallel to whales. When whales are travelling close to shore, avoid crowding them near shore or coming between the whales and shore.
4 Approach no closer than 100 metres and idle along at the speed of the whales, or shift your motor into neutral. Keep noise levels down — no horns, whistles, or racing motors. Start your motor only after the whales are more than 100 metres from your vessel. Leave the area slowly, gradually accelerating when more than 300 metres from the whales.
5 Limit the time spent with any group of whales to less than 30 minutes at a time when within 100 to 200 metres of the whales.
6 Be considerate of other whale watchers so that all have a chance to view without disturbance. If several boats are following one group of whales, check the surrounding areas with binoculars to see if other groups are nearby. If possible, decrease boat congestion by following an unwatched group.
7 If a group of whales changes direction repeatedly or changes behaviours quickly (e.g., from slow travelling to fast travelling), these are signs of possible disturbance and the group should be left alone.

### Robson Bight (Michael Bigg) Ecological Reserve

Robson Bight is located on the typical foraging route of resident whales in Johnstone Strait and is the site of several beaches that are frequently used by these whales for rubbing (see map, p. 46). The Robson Bight (Michael Bigg) Ecological Reserve was established in 1982 by BC Parks as a sanctuary for killer whales and to protect these important rubbing beaches. It includes 1,248 hectares of marine area and 505 hectares of upland buffer zone.
Ecological reserves are intended for conservation, research, and educational purposes, and are not intended for recreation. At Robson Bight, a number of restrictions are currently in place to better protect the area, and further restrictions may be applied as required. The area is monitored daily during summer months by wardens who can provide detailed information to boaters. The key restrictions are as follows:

1 Land access is now restricted in the ecological reserve and the landing of vessels is prohibited.
2 Recreational activities, such as whale watching, should not take place in the reserve. Boats requiring sheltered waters, such as canoes and kayaks, should cross over to West Cracroft Island, where there are good anchorages and camping is permitted.
3 Commercial fishing activity in the reserve is currently under review.
4 As with all ecological reserves, camping, campfires, and discharge of firearms are prohibited.

### Regulations and Licensing

In Canada, the Department of Fisheries and Oceans is responsible for the management and protection of marine mammals, including killer whales. In the United States, the responsible agency is the National Marine Fisheries Service. In both countries, regulations specifically prohibit disturbance of whales. Infractions are subject to fines and/or imprisonment.

Activities such as research or commercial photography may require a license or permit to approach whales. Individuals wishing to carry out such activities should contact the Department of Fisheries and Oceans in Canada, or the National Marine Fisheries Service in the US, to ensure that their proposed activity is permissible and to determine whether or not they will require a scientific permit. For research activities that may require entry of the Robson Bight (Michael Bigg) Ecological Reserve, researchers must contact BC Parks.

A-Clan

# C1 Pod
## C6 Subpod

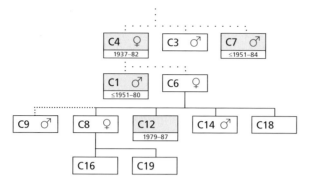

**C3**  ♂ ≤1952

**The C5 and C6 subpods share a dialect that is very similar to that of D1 pod. The two subpods are mostly encountered separately – in only about one-quarter of encounters in the 1990s have the two groups been together.**

**C6**  ♀ 1955

*The dorsal fin of the bull C9 sustained a major injury in 1993. Likely caused by a bite from another killer whale, or possibly a gunshot, this kind of injury can take many years to heal, during which time the fin may continue to collapse.*

**C9**  ♂ 1971

**C8**  ♀ 1975

**C14**  ♂ 1985

**C18**  1991

**C16**  1989

**C19**  1991

# C1 Pod
## C5 Subpod

**C5**  ♀ 1924

The matriarch, C5, is most likely the mother of C11, widely known as the whale "Namu." This bull was captured near the town of Namu on the central BC coast in 1965 and transported to Seattle in a floating pen. "Namu" became known around the world through magazine articles, books, and a movie.

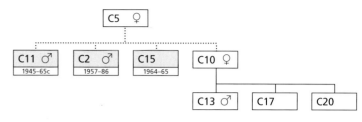

**C10**  ♀ 1971

**C13** ♂ 1985   **C17** 1989   **C20** 1993

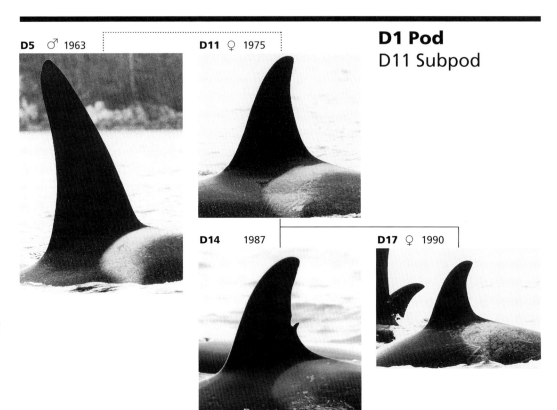

**D5** ♂ 1963

**D11** ♀ 1975

# D1 Pod
## D11 Subpod

**D14** 1987

**D17** ♀ 1990

D1 pod is usually quite common in Johnstone Strait, but only occasionally visited this area in the early 1990s. The two sub-pods, D7 and D11, typically travel together (in about 75% of encounters).

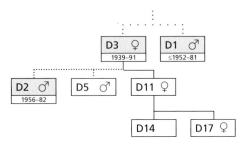

D3 ♀ 1939–91    D1 ♂ ≤1952–81

D2 ♂ 1956–82    D5 ♂    D11 ♀

D14    D17 ♀

# D1 Pod
## D7 Subpod

**D7**  ♀  1941

**D8**  ♀  1967

**D9**  ♀  1971

**D10**  1978

**D13**  ♂  1984

**D12**  1982

**D15**  1987

*D10 has a small hole through her dorsal fin, apparently caused by a bullet.*

*D9 can be easily confused with the cow C10 (p. 59), as they have very similar dorsal-fin nicks.*

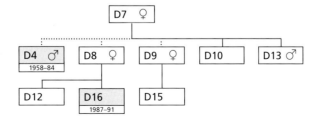

# H1 Pod
## H6 Subpod

**H6** ♀ 1942

H1 pod is currently considered to consist of a single subpod, but this may change in the near future. Recently, H3 and her offspring have been seen apart from the rest of the H group on a few occasions, and H6 and H2 have also been seen travelling separately from the rest of the pod.

H1 pod has a very distinctive dialect that is related to the those of B1, I1, I2, and I18 pods.

**H3** ♀ 1959

**H2** ♂ 1965

**H5** ♀ 1973

**H4** ♂ 1974

**H7** ♂ 1981

**H8** 1986

**H9** ♀ 1988

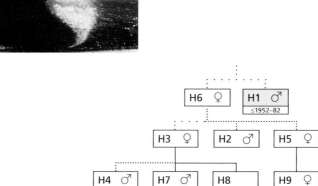

| H6 ♀ | H1 ♂ ≤1952–82 | |
|---|---|---|
| H3 ♀ | H2 ♂ | H5 ♀ |
| H4 ♂   H7 ♂   H8 | | H9 ♀ |

# I1 Pod
## I1 Subpod

**I3**  ♂ ≤1954

**I1**  ♀ 1952

I1 pod is one of the least commonly encountered northern resident groups, having been seen only 27 times in 20 years. It appears to spend more time off northern Vancouver Island and along the central coast of BC.

*I3's dorsal fin slowly collapsed over several years in the late 1970s and early 1980s. The cause of this anomaly is unknown. Several other whales in this and other regions have been observed with the same fin condition.*

**I19**  ♀ 1968

**I23**  ♂ 1973

**I40**  ♀ 1980

**I54**  ♀ 1983

**I56**  1986

**\***  **I70**  1993

**I69**  1992

**I71**  ♀ 1993

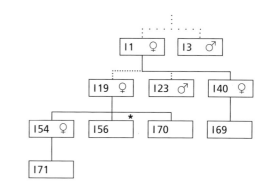

# I2 Pod
## I2 Subpod

I2 ♀ 1936

*The I2 subpod may well be reduced to two whales, as the bulls I8 and I14 were missing in 1993. I5 has one of the most distinctive dorsal fins on the coast.*

# I2 Pod
## I22 Subpod

*The I22 subpod spends a good deal of time apart from the matriarch, I2. As in other groups, this may be due to the high proportion of males in the I2 subpod. Two of these bulls, however, were missing in 1993.*

I14 ♂ ≤1954    **\***    I5 ♂ ≤1954     I8 ♂ 1962    **\***    I22 ♀ 1965

I39 ♂ 1980      I55 1987

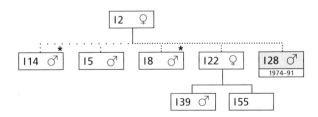

I18 pod is the least-known northern resident pod, having been seen only 23 times during the study. It is a burgeoning group, however, increasing from 5 whales in 1975 to 19 (two of which were missing in 1993). Acoustically, I18 pod is very closely related to I1 and I2 pods.

# I18 Pod
## I17 Subpod

**I17** ♀ 1959

**I26** ♀ 1975 **I38** 1979 **I50** 1982 **I57** 1989

**I60** 1987

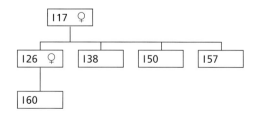

```
        ┌──────────┐
        │ I17   ♀  │
        └──────────┘
   ┌───────┬──────┬──────┐
┌──────┐ ┌──────┐ ┌──────┐ ┌──────┐
│I26 ♀ │ │ I38  │ │ I50  │ │ I57  │
└──────┘ └──────┘ └──────┘ └──────┘
   │
┌──────┐
│ I60  │
└──────┘
```

# I18 Pod
## I18 Subpod

I18 ♀ 1947

I20 ♀ 1964

I7 ♀ 1968 *

I21 1979

I52 1986

I66 1991

I48 1983

I59 1988

| 149 ♂ 1976 | 124 1980 | 153 1986 | 158 1989 | * 173 1992 |

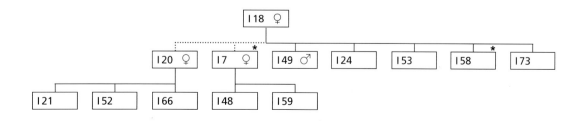

```
                    ┌──────────┐
                    │ 118  ♀   │
                    └────┬─────┘
      ┌·········┌────────┼────────┬────────┬────────┬────────┐
      *         │        │        │        │        *        │
  ┌───────┐ ┌───────┐ ┌───────┐ ┌─────┐ ┌─────┐ ┌─────┐ ┌─────┐
  │ 120 ♀ │ │ 17  ♀ │ │ 149 ♂ │ │ 124 │ │ 153 │ │ 158 │ │ 173 │
  └───┬───┘ └───┬───┘ └───────┘ └─────┘ └─────┘ └─────┘ └─────┘
 ┌────┼────┐ ┌──┴──┐
┌───┐┌───┐┌───┐┌───┐┌───┐
│121││152││166││148││159│
└───┘└───┘└───┘└───┘└───┘
```

# G1 Pod
## G4 Subpod

**G4** ♀ 1948

**G6** ♂ 1965

**G26** ♂ 1970

*G6's distinctive saddle patch pigmentation is referred to as an "open saddle." This type of saddle pattern is far more common among southern residents than northerns.*

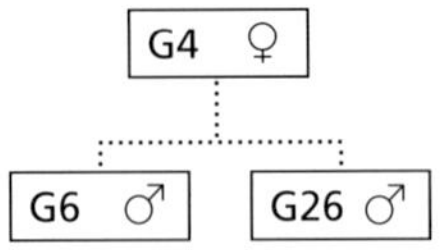

# G1 Pod
## G3 Subpod

**G3** ♀ 1956

With 28 members, G1 pod is the largest northern resident pod. It frequently splits into smaller units, comprising five subpods.

**G20** ♀ 1972

**G19** ♂ 1976

**G37** 1984

**G48** 1990

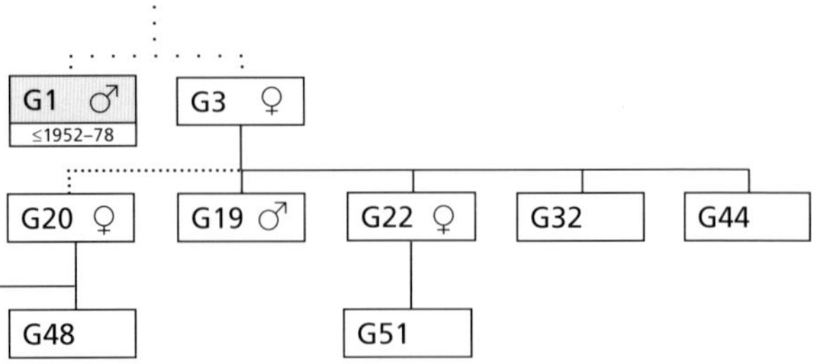

```
        G4  ♀
         |
   ┌─────┴─────┐
 G6  ♂     G26  ♂
```

```
          G1  ♂     G3  ♀
          ≤1952–78    |
      ┌────────┬──────┴──┬───────┬───────┐
   G20  ♀   G19  ♂   G22  ♀   G32    G44
   ┌──┴──┐              |
 G37    G48            G51
```

The G-clan contains four of the most rapidly growing resident pods. The clan has doubled in size over 18 years, from 33 whales in 1975 to 66 in 1993. Although members of all three northern resident clans have been observed on the west coast of Vancouver Island, G-clan groups are seen in this area most often.

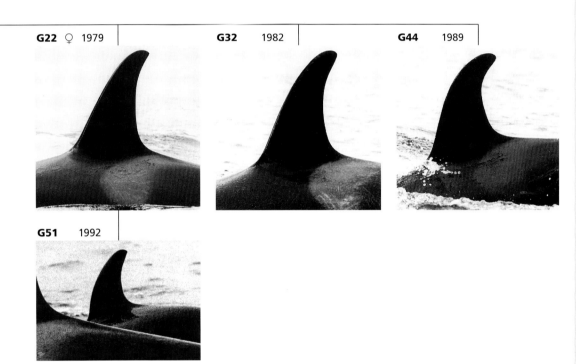

G22 ♀ 1979  G32 1982  G44 1989

G51 1992

**Key**

A1 ♀
1927–74
Deceased killer whale with estimated or known birth date and date of death

\* missing in 1993

c live captured

*Genealogical relationship:*

———— Positive

················ Probable

· · · · · · · Possible

### *Orcinus orca:* The Killer Dolphin

Although killer whales are found in all the world's oceans, only a single species, *Orcinus orca*, is recognized. Over the past two centuries, a number of different taxonomic forms of killer whale have been proposed, some with interesting names, such as *Orca gladiator*, but these have not been accepted in the scientific community. Recently, Russian biologists suggested that a new species, which they named *Orcinus glacialis*, existed in Antarctic seas. This proposed species was characterized as having a smaller size and a variety of differences in diet, reproduction, appearance, and behaviour, but this classification, too, has not met with general acceptance. More likely, such variations represent racial differences, such as those seen locally between residents and transients.

*Orcinus orca* is the largest member of the Family Delphinidae, which includes all the world's marine dolphins. For this reason, its common name might be more appropriately the "killer dolphin," but its large size has led to it being called a whale. The distinction between "dolphin" and "whale" is not a scientific one, but relates mostly to relative size, much like the distinction between "boat" and "ship."

Because the species has such a cosmopolitan distribution, it has many common names in different parts of the globe. In some Native cultures, it is known as:

*max'inux* (northern Vancouver Island Kwakiutl)
*ska-ana* (Haida of the Queen Charlotte Islands)
*arluq* (eastern Arctic Inuit)
*dukulad* (Ainos of the Kuril Islands)
*shamanaj* (Yahgan of Tierra del Fuego, South America)

In other languages, it is called:

*épaulard* (French)
*hahyrningur* (Icelandic)
*shachi* (Japanese)
*kasatka* (Russian)
*schwertwal* or *mörderwal* (German)
*spekkhugger* (Norwegian)

Many of these common names refer to the killer whale's deserved – but sometimes exaggerated – reputation as the top predator in the sea, and reflect fear or respect. Even the widely used *orca*, has sinister connotations, as it is derived from the species' scientific name, which uses the Latin word *orcinus*, meaning "of or belonging to the kingdom of the dead." For many years, the species was called *blackfish* by coastal mariners and fishermen in BC, despite the fact that they are black and white. Within the English-speaking scientific community, "killer whale" is the common name used most often today.

# G1 Pod
## G17 Subpod

**G17** ♀ 1948

**G25** ♀ 1975

**G23** ♀ 1980

**G38** 1986

**G40** 1987

**G50** 1991

*The link between cow G23 and calf G50 is based on one poor encounter with this subpod, and thus it is only "probable." Future encounters should confirm this mother/off-spring relationship.*

# G1 Pod
## G16 Subpod

**G11** ♂ 1962

*Both the G16 and G24 subpods, as well as the G8 subpod in G12 pod, lost their matriarchs in 1989.*

| G17 ♀ | G7 ♂ |
|---|---|
| | ≤1952–81 |

| G9 ♂ | G25 ♀ | G23 ♀ | G38 |
|---|---|---|---|
| 1965–89 | | | |

| G40 | G50 |
|---|---|

| G18 ♀ |
|---|
| 1945–89 |

| G11 ♂ | G16 ♀ | G31 |
|---|---|---|

| G39 | G52 |
|---|---|

**G16** ♀ 1971　　**G31** 1981

**G39** 1986　　**G52** 1992

# G1 Pod
## G24 Subpod

**G24** ♀ 1941

**G5** ♂ 1958　　　　\*　**G29** ♀ 1970

**G45** 1988　　**G46** 1991

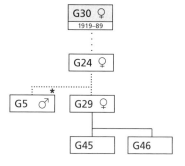

G30 ♀
1919–89

G24 ♀

G5 ♂ 　\*　 G29 ♀

G45　　G46

# G12 Pod
## G8 Subpod

G1 and G12 pods share the same distinctive dialect, indicating close relatedness. About one-half of their call repertoire is shared with I11 and I31 pods, suggesting a more distant relationship with those groups.

**G8** ♀ 1971

**G27** ♀ 1973

**G33** ♂ 1978

**G35** 1985

**G47** 1990

**G41** 1987

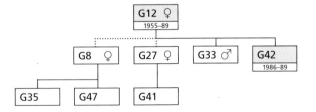

## G12 Pod
## G2 Subpod

**G2**  ♀  1961

**G34**  ♀  1977

**G28**  1981

**G43**  1989

**G49**  1990

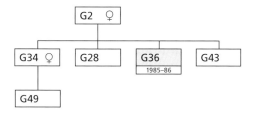

G2 ♀

G34 ♀ — G28 — G36 (1985–86) — G43

G49

G-Clan

# I 11 Pod
## I 11 Subpod

**I 11** ♀ 1954

**I 12** ♀ 1970

**I 13** ♀ 1974

**I 37** ♂ 1979

**I 42** 1983

**I 64** 1990

**I 47** 1985

*The cow I12 and her juvenile I47 have distinctive "open" saddles. Within the northern resident community, such saddle patterns are found mostly in G-clan whales.*

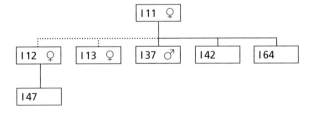

## Communication and Echolocation

Like all members of the dolphin family, killer whales rely heavily on underwater sound for both navigation and communication, and with good reason. Sound is by far the most efficient and reliable medium for collecting sensory information about a whale's surroundings and for social communication with other whales. The whales' eyesight is good, but underwater visibility is usually less than 50 metres, and at night it is negligible. Underwater sound, on the other hand, travels farther and faster than it does in air, and is equally effective day or night.

By forcing air through structures in the nasal passage beneath the blowhole, a killer whale can generate ultrasonic clicks less than a millisecond in duration, long canary-like whistles, or loud, complex calls that may be heard for 10 kilometres underwater. A special body of fat within the melon, the fleshy bulge atop the animal's head, has acoustic properties that focus the higher-frequency sounds into a directional beam ahead of the whale. Killer whales can hear with exceptional sensitivity and directionality. Incoming sound is received mostly through the whale's lower jaw, then is conducted directly to the middle ear.

Lowering an underwater microphone, or hydrophone, into the water near killer whales provides a means of eavesdropping on their acoustic world. When listening to a group of resident killer whales, one usually hears staccato snaps, clicks, and pops of echolocation, punctuated every so often by strident, often metallic-sounding calls being exchanged within the group. The echolocation signals produced by the whales are referred to as "click trains," which are short-duration pulses given in repetitive series that may last for 10 seconds or more. Echoes from these clicks allow the animals to form an acoustical image of their surroundings. The repetition rate of clicks varies from a few to more than 200 clicks per second, probably in relation to the range of the target being acoustically examined. Slow click trains are probably used for navigation and orientation to distant objects, such as seafloor features or other whales. Higher repetition rates seem to be used to investigate closer objects at ranges of 10 metres or less.

The signals used for social communication within and between pods consist of calls and whistles. Calls are more common than whistles, dominating vocal exchanges in most contexts. Typically less than two seconds long, calls are made up of bursts of pulses generated at rates of up to several thousand per second. Such pulse bursts produce high-pitched squeals and screams not unlike the sounds made by rusty hinges on a quickly closing door. By varying the timing and frequency structure of these bursts, the whales can generate a variety of complex signals.

Most calls produced by resident pods can be classified by ear or with the aid of sound spectrum analyzer into a number of distinctive categories, or types of *discrete calls*. Each resident pod has a repertoire of about a dozen different discrete call types, although some have as few as 7 and others have as many as 17 call types. Each whale seems to share the entire call repertoire of its pod. These calls appear to serve generally as contact signals, coordinating group behaviour and keeping pod members in touch when they are out of sight of each other. While spread out during foraging, the whales regularly exchange sounds, 90-95% of which are from their repertoire of discrete calls. Most calls contain sudden shifts or rapid sweeps in pitch, which give them distinctive qualities recognizable over distance and background noise.

As described in "Dialects and Population Identity" (p. 21), the call repertoire of each resident pod has unique features that allow the group to be identified acoustically. These dialects may enhance the contact function of the calls by acting like an acoustic "family badge," allowing individuals to easily differentiate the calls of their fellow pod members from those of other whales. Dialects may also serve as indicators of relatedness of pods, and might thus have some role in determining association or mating patterns.

It is not yet clear why pods have so many calls in their repertoires or whether any call has a specific meaning. Different calls do not appear to be given in sequences that resemble a syntax, such as in human languages. Rather, call types seem to be contagious — if a whale emits a particular call, others in the pod often respond with the same call type before moving on to another. No call appears to be associated exclusively with any particular activity or behaviour. However, certain calls in a pod's repertoire do tend to be given more often in some circumstances, such as resting or socializing, than in others.

Most likely, the emotional state of an individual is reflected in the call types it chooses to use, and also in the way each call is given. For example, when whales are excited, they will often increase the pitch and shorten the duration of a call from its standard format. It is also probable that each whale produces calls in a consistent but subtly different way from others in its pod, thus encoding its identity in the signal. With this communication system, resident whales seem able to transmit their individual and pod identity, location, and mood to others in their pod, thereby maintaining the behavioural coordination, cohesion, and integrity of the group.

# I 11 Pod
## I 15 Subpod

**I 15** ♀ 1952

**I 16** ♀ 1968

**I 27** ♀ 1974

**I 4** ♀ 1980

**I 43** ♂ 1983

**I 51** 1986

**I 72** 1993

**I 63** 1990

I4 and I41 are twins born to the cow I15 in 1980. Twinning is very rare, but may take place more often than we observe. As most calves are born in winter and fall, one or both twin calves may die before they are identified.

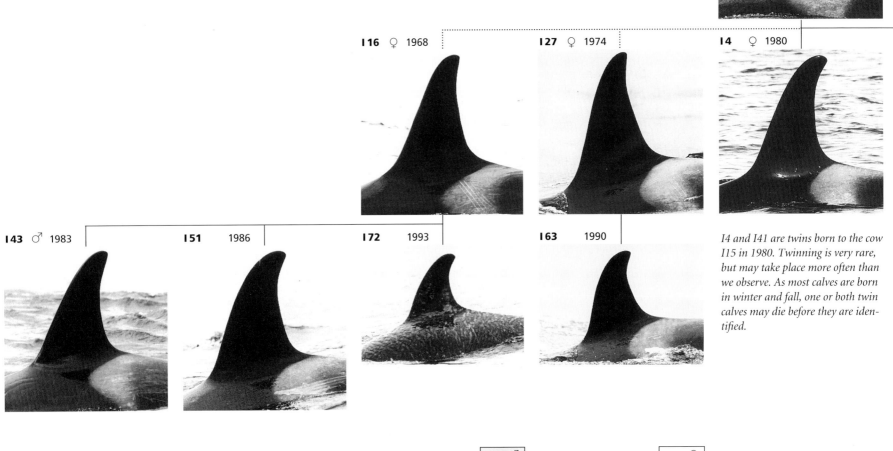

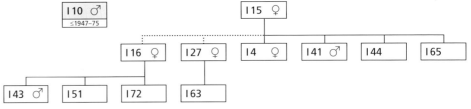

**I41** ♂ 1980  **I44** 1985  **I65** 1990

**Wanted: ID photos**

If you have taken photographs from which individual whales can be identified, you may have useful scientific information that could assist our ongoing research program. Photos of killer whales in remote locations are particularly useful, as they may reveal a new group or extend the range of a group already known. Areas for which we especially need information include the west coasts of Washington State and Vancouver Island, areas north of Vancouver Island, the Queen Charlotte Islands, and any offshore waters. Photos taken in any location prior to 1970 are also of considerable value to us in studies on longevity in these whales.

If you have photos that you believe may be useful, please send them to us. The photographs and identifications will be returned, usually in a week or two. Each set of photos should include the name of the photographer, date, locations, and the number of whales present. Photographs can be sent to:

Marine Mammal Research
Department of Fisheries and Oceans
Pacific Biological Station
Nanaimo, BC  V9R 5K6
Phone: (604) 756-7245

or

Center for Whale Research
P.O. Box 1577
Friday Harbor, WA 98250
Phone: (206) 378-5835

# 131 Pod
## 131 Subpod

**131** ♀ 1946

*The cow I31 and her son I32 share similar, unusually shaped saddle patches.*

**132** ♂ 1963

**135** ♀ 1974

**136** 1980

**146** ♂ 1985

**168** 1992

**167** 1991

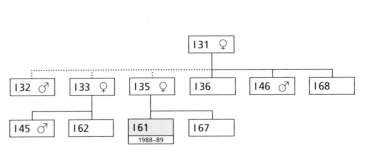

# I31 Pod
## I33 Subpod

**I33** ♀ 1970

*I33 and her offspring form one of the few groups that regularly separate from the matriarch's subpod. The I22 subpod (I2 pod, p. 64) is a similar example.*

**I45** ♂ 1985

**I62** 1988

## Changing Features of Fins and Saddles

Although a photograph can provide a reliable identification of a whale, the appearance of an individual's dorsal fin can change dramatically over the years. As a whale grows, the shape and size of its fin changes, especially in males, whose adult fin height can be ten times its height at birth. Over time, dorsal fins also acquire new nicks, tears, and gouges, and saddle patches often receive new scars from teeth rakes and other natural causes. It is for this reason that we photograph whales at regular intervals, ideally every year, so that such changes can be catalogued. This is especially important over the first few years of a whale's life, because a juvenile's fin and saddle can change quickly from being nondescript to distinctively marked.

The changes in the fin and saddle of some whales are far more prominent than in others. The whale H4 is a good example of an individual whose appearance has changed significantly over its life. Shown here is a series of identification photographs spanning H4's growth from calf to mature bull.

**G-Clan**

July 1975

July 1980

July 1982

July 1985

August 1986

August 1993

## R1 Pod
### R2 Subpod

**R2** ♀ 1938

**R6** ♂ ≤1954

**R3** ♂ 1956

**R12** ♂ 1966

R6's dorsal fin has a forward hook, an attribute sometimes seen in old bulls. Other whales with this type of fin profile include B1 (p. 56), C3 (p. 58), and R1 (p. 82).

## R1 Pod
### R5 Subpod

*Having no living mother, the bull R6 frequently wanders from the subpod for significant periods of time. The apparent brothers, R14 and R15 (R9 subpod), who similarly have no living mother, also occasionally travel apart from their group.*

**R4** ♀ 1964

**R22** ♂ 1984

**R26** 1988

**R28** 1992

### Key

| A1 ♀ | Deceased killer whale with esti-mated or known birth date and date of death |

1927–74

\* missing in 1993

c live captured

*Genealogical relationship:*

——— Positive

·············· Probable

· · · · · · Possible

| R2 ♀ | R6 ♂ |

| R3 ♂ | R12 ♂ |

**R5** ♀ 1948

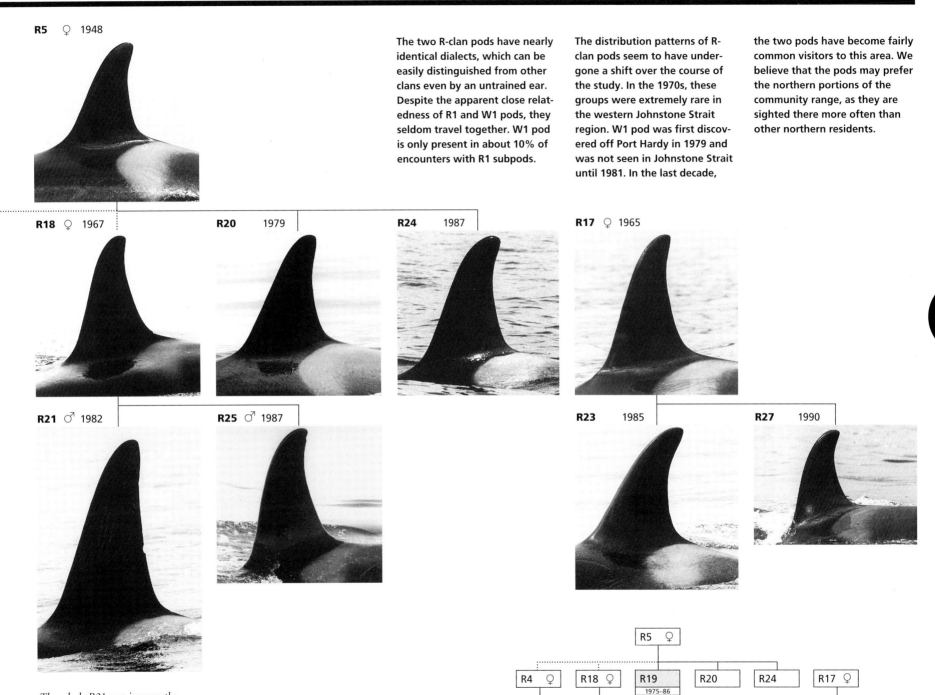

The two R-clan pods have nearly identical dialects, which can be easily distinguished from other clans even by an untrained ear. Despite the apparent close relatedness of R1 and W1 pods, they seldom travel together. W1 pod is only present in about 10% of encounters with R1 subpods.

The distribution patterns of R-clan pods seem to have undergone a shift over the course of the study. In the 1970s, these groups were extremely rare in the western Johnstone Strait region. W1 pod was first discovered off Port Hardy in 1979 and was not seen in Johnstone Strait until 1981. In the last decade, the two pods have become fairly common visitors to this area. We believe that the pods may prefer the northern portions of the community range, as they are sighted there more often than other northern residents.

**R18** ♀ 1967

**R20** 1979

**R24** 1987

**R17** ♀ 1965

**R21** ♂ 1982

**R25** ♂ 1987

**R23** 1985

**R27** 1990

*The whale R21 was incorrectly assigned as an offspring of the cow R4 in the 1987 catalogue. Further encounters with the subpod confirmed that he is actually a son of R18.*

R-Clan

# R1 Pod
## R9 Subpod

**R9**  ♀  1923

*The dorsal fin of the matriarch R9 has a sharp bend to the left near its tip.*

**R7**  ♀  1944

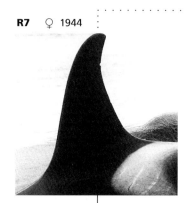

**R13**  ♀  1979

**R1**  ♂  ≤1954

**R14**  ♂  ≤1954

**R15**  ♂  1963

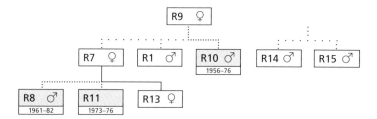

# W1 Pod
## W3 Subpod

**W3**  ♀  1940

**W2**  ♂  1960

**W5**  ♂  1974

W1 is the smallest resident pod, with only three members. It is comprised of a single matrilineal group that will in time die out, as W3 is now post-reproductive.

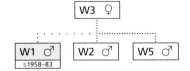

| W3 ♀ |
|------|

| W1 ♂ | W2 ♂ | W5 ♂ |
|------|------|------|
| ≤1958–83 | | |

## Killer Whales, Ships, and Care-Giving Behaviour

Killer whales are clearly very accustomed to swimming close to power boats and ships without striking and injuring themselves on the vessels' propellers. But collisions sometimes take place and may cause serious injury or death. Two whales, the northern residents A1 and A9, were both apparently injured in this way, but survived. The wounds on these old females – both of whom are now dead – were fully healed at the start of our study in the early 1970s. The whale A1 was known as "Stubbs" because all that remained of her dorsal fin was a ragged stump about half the normal height (see photo, p. 42). The other cow, A9, the matriarch of A5 pod, had major pieces of flesh missing from her dorsal ridge between her dorsal fin and tail flukes. Although healed, the wounds extended almost to the backbone in several places.

One often wonders how whales can survive such major physical trauma. It is very likely that without the strong drive of these animals to aid distressed companions, most would die. The following is an account of a collision between a ship and a killer whale that demonstrates the persistence of the whales in helping one of their pod mates. It is drawn from a letter written by Captain D. Manuel of the M/V *Comox Queen*, a ship that is part of the BC Ferries fleet. The ship was en route from Comox to Powell River on 26 December 1973, when it encountered killer whales:

*The Quartermaster and I were discussing some subject or other and watching for drift. There was quite a lot of it around, due to the high tides at that time.*

*At 3:45 there was a crunch at the after end of the ship, as if we had struck a small log. I went and looked out the window at the back of the wheelhouse and noticed a reddish-brown discolouration in our wake. My first impression was that we had struck a butt-end of a dead-head just below the surface of the water. Then four killer whales surfaced about two to three ship lengths astern.*

*The first thing I noticed about these four surfacing whales was that one was bleeding profusely. I told the Quartermaster to bring the ship hard around and we steamed up to within ten feet of the whales. The pod consisted of a bull, cow and two calves. It was one of the calves that had been struck by the ship's propellers. It was a very sad scene to see. The cow and the bull cradled the injured calf between them to prevent it from turning upside-down. Occasionally the bull would lose its position and the calf would roll over on its side. When this occurred the slashes caused by our propeller were quite visible. The bull, when this happened, would make a tight circle, submerge, and rise slowly beside the calf, righting it, and then proceed with the diving and surfacing. While this was going on the other calf stayed right behind the injured one.*

*We stayed with the whales for about ten to fifteen minutes; there was no fear of the ship being too close (about ten feet at times). I felt at the time that there was very little we could do to alleviate the obvious pain and suffering that was taking place and that the calf could not survive for too long.*

It appears that the young whale did live for at least fifteen days. We later received a report from a resident of Powell River, who, on 10 January 1974, observed "two whales supporting a third one, preventing it from turning over." We do not know whether the whale survived after this, as we received no further sightings or photographs from which we could identify the individual. We suspect, however, that it might have been a young A5-pod whale identified as A21, which was last seen in 1973. Serious injuries from collisions with vessels are probably rare events, as none have been observed among the known whales in British Columbia and Washington State during the past twenty years.

Greg Davies

R-Clan

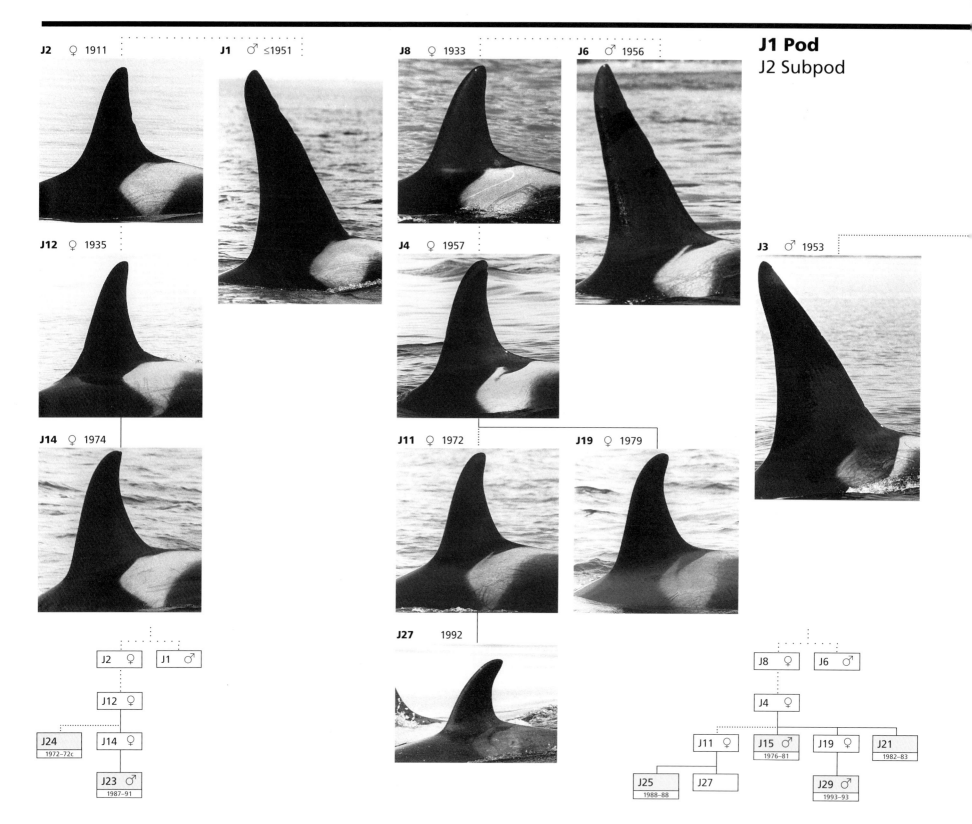

**J2** ♀ 1911

**J1** ♂ ≤1951

**J8** ♀ 1933

**J6** ♂ 1956

# J1 Pod
## J2 Subpod

**J12** ♀ 1935

**J4** ♀ 1957

**J3** ♂ 1953

**J14** ♀ 1974

**J11** ♀ 1972

**J19** ♀ 1979

**J27** 1992

| J2 ♀ | J1 ♂ |
|------|------|

| J12 ♀ |
|-------|

| J24 | J14 ♀ |
|------|--------|
| 1972–72c | |

| J23 ♂ |
|--------|
| 1987–91 |

| J8 ♀ | J6 ♂ |
|------|------|

| J4 ♀ |
|------|

| J11 ♀ | J15 ♂ | J19 ♀ | J21 |
|-------|--------|--------|------|
| | 1976–81 | | 1982–83 |

| J25 | J27 |
|------|------|
| 1988–88 | |

| J29 ♂ |
|--------|
| 1993–93 |

J1 pod is one of the most cohesive resident pods, rarely splitting into separate groups. It is also one of the best-known pods. Of the three southern resident pods, J1 spends the most time in the waters of San Juan Island and the Gulf Islands.

J1 pod's vocal dialect has changed little over the years. Canadian Navy recordings of killer whales near Victoria in the late 1950s contain the J1 dialect in generally the same form as today. In 1964, the first killer whale ever displayed in captivity, "Moby Doll," was captured at Saturna Island. Recordings of this whale's dialect indicate that it was from J1 pod.

**J5** ♀ 1938

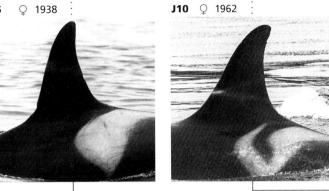

**J10** ♀ 1962

**J16** ♀ 1972

**J17** ♀ 1977

**J18** ♂ 1978

**J20** ♀ 1981

**J22** ♀ 1985

**J26** ♂ 1992

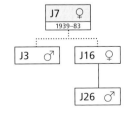

**J28** 1993

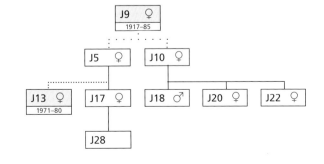

## Key

| A1 ♀ | Deceased killer whale with esti-mated or known birth date and date of death |
| --- | --- |

1927–74

* missing in 1993

c live captured

*Genealogical relationship:*

——— Positive

............ Probable

· · · · · · Possible

**J7** ♀
1939–83

**J3** ♂   **J16** ♀

**J26** ♂

**J9** ♀
1917–85

**J5** ♀   **J10** ♀

**J13** ♀   **J17** ♀   **J18** ♂   **J20** ♀   **J22** ♀
1971–80

**J28**

# K1 Pod
## K7 Subpod

Highly distinctive, "open" saddle patches are far more common among southern residents than northerns. These patterns can be a very useful aid to visual identification of individuals. It should be noted that the pattern on a whale's right side often differs from the left side.

**K7** ♀ 1910

*The whale K7 is estimated to have been born in 1910, which makes her the oldest in the resident population and at the maximum theoretical age. It should be noted, however, that the uncertainty of such estimates increases with age, and she may be as much as 12 years younger. More details on longevity calculations are given on pp. 44-45.*

*In the first encounters with K1 pod each year, usually during late spring, K7 subpod is typically seen without K18 subpod. By early summer, however, the two subpods reunite and tend to remain together for the remainder of the summer.*

**K3** ♀ 1954

**K11** ♀ 1933

**K1** ♂ 1955

*The two distinctive nicks in the dorsal fin of bull K1 were made by Michael Bigg in October 1973, when the whale was temporarily held captive at Pedder Bay, near Victoria. The whale was also fitted with a radio-tracking tag attached at the base of the dorsal fin, so that he could be followed after release. Unfortunately, the signal was lost eight hours following release because of radio interference. When K1 was sighted again several months later, the radio tag had fallen off – as it was designed to do after its batteries were exhausted – but the two fin nicks remained. That these nicks are basically unchanged 20 years later illustrates the permanence of such injuries involving tissue loss.*

**K14** ♀ 1977

**K16** ♀ 1985

**K13** ♀ 1972

**K26** 1993

**K20** 1986

**K25** 1991

**K4** ♀ 1933

**K12** ♀ 1971

**K22** 1987

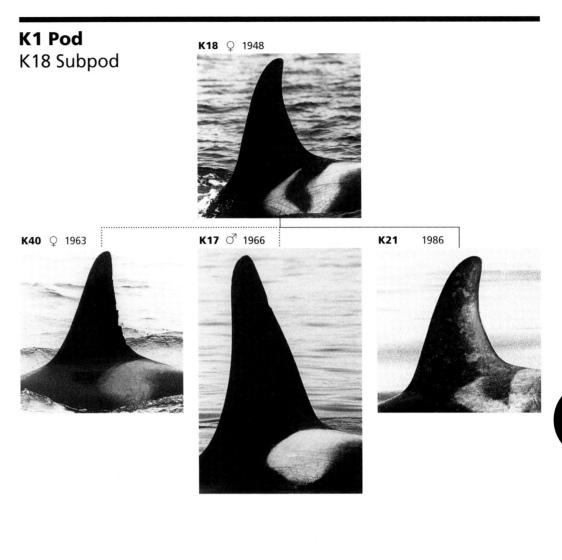

**K18** ♀ 1948

**K40** ♀ 1963

**K17** ♂ 1966

**K21** 1986

J-Clan

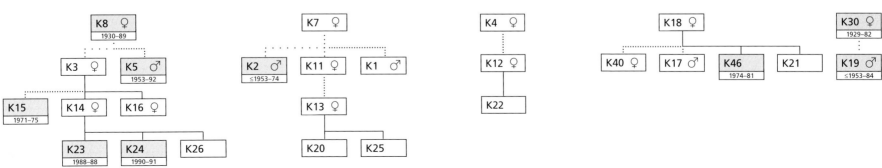

| K8 ♀ |
|---|
| 1930–89 |

| K3 ♀ | K5 ♂ |
|---|---|
| | 1953–92 |

| K15 | K14 ♀ | K16 ♀ |
|---|---|---|
| 1971–75 | | |

| K23 | K24 | K26 |
|---|---|---|
| 1988–88 | 1990–91 | |

| K7 ♀ |
|---|

| K2 ♂ | K11 ♀ | K1 ♂ |
|---|---|---|
| ≤1953–74 | | |

| K13 ♀ |
|---|

| K20 | K25 |
|---|---|

| K4 ♀ |
|---|

| K12 ♀ |
|---|

| K22 |
|---|

| K18 ♀ |
|---|

| K40 ♀ | K17 ♂ | K46 | K21 |
|---|---|---|---|
| | | 1974–81 | |

| K30 ♀ |
|---|
| 1929–82 |

| K19 ♂ |
|---|
| ≤1953–84 |

# L1 Pod
## L12 Subpod

L1 pod spends more time in "outside" waters – in western Juan de Fuca Strait and off the west coast of Vancouver Island – than does either J1 or K1 pods.

**L12**  ♀  1933

**L11**  ♀  1957

**L10**  ♂  1959

*Over the last few years, the L12 matrilineal group has been seen travelling increasingly apart from the L28 and L32 matrilineal groups, although the three still tend to swim in close association while resting.*

**L42**  ♂  1973

**L41**  ♂  1977

**L77**  1987

**L75**  ♀  1986

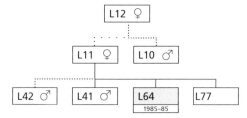

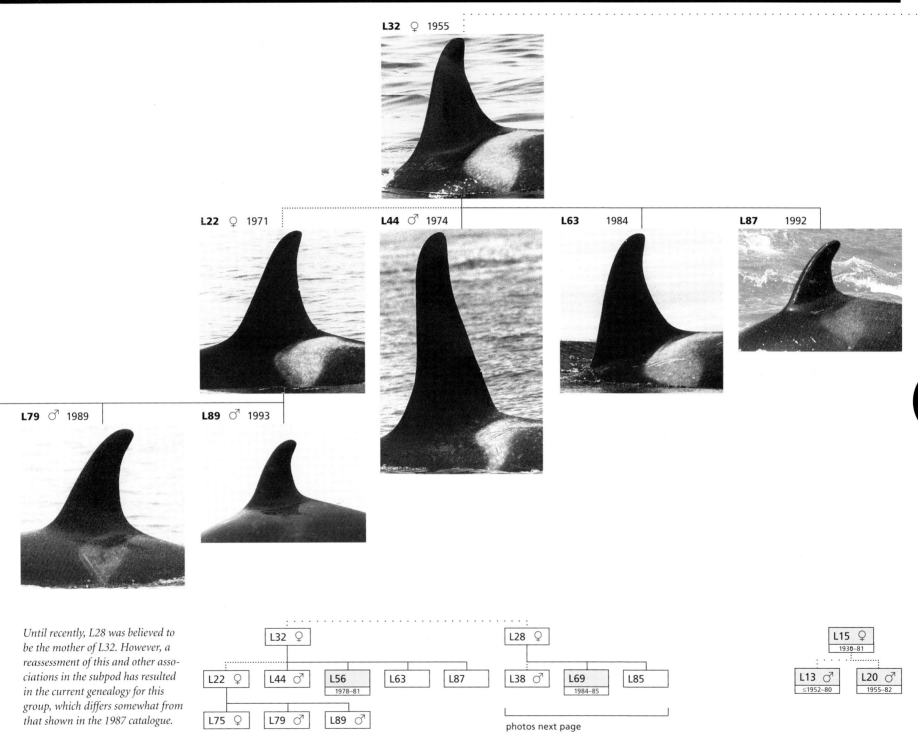

**L32** ♀ 1955

**L22** ♀ 1971

**L44** ♂ 1974

**L63** 1984

**L87** 1992

**L79** ♂ 1989

**L89** ♂ 1993

*Until recently, L28 was believed to be the mother of L32. However, a reassessment of this and other associations in the subpod has resulted in the current genealogy for this group, which differs somewhat from that shown in the 1987 catalogue.*

| L32 ♀ | | | L28 ♀ | | | L15 ♀ |
|---|---|---|---|---|---|---|
| | | | | | | 1930–81 |

| L22 ♀ | L44 ♂ | L56 | L63 | L87 | L38 ♂ | L69 | L85 | L13 ♂ | L20 ♂ |
|---|---|---|---|---|---|---|---|---|---|
| | | 1978–81 | | | | 1984–85 | | ≤1952–80 | 1955–82 |

| L75 ♀ | L79 ♂ | L89 ♂ |
|---|---|---|

photos next page

## L1 Pod
## L12 Subpod, continued

**L28** ♀ 1949

**L38** ♂ 1965

**L85** 1991

## L1 Pod
## L25 Subpod

**L7** ♀ 1961

**L43** ♀ 1972

**L53** ♀ 1977

**L72** 1986

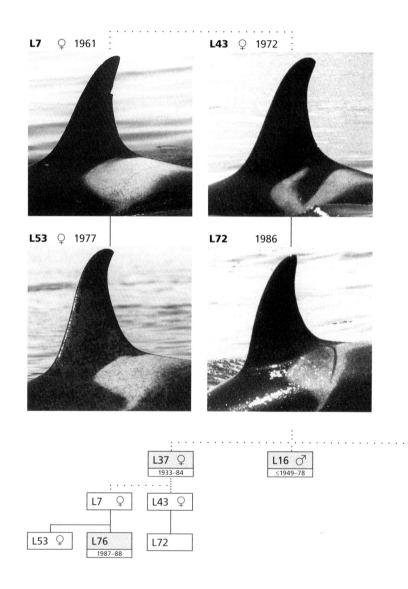

| L37 ♀ | | L16 ♂ |
| 1933–84 | | ≤1949–78 |

| L7 ♀ | L43 ♀ |

| L53 ♀ | L76 | L72 |
| | 1987–88 | |

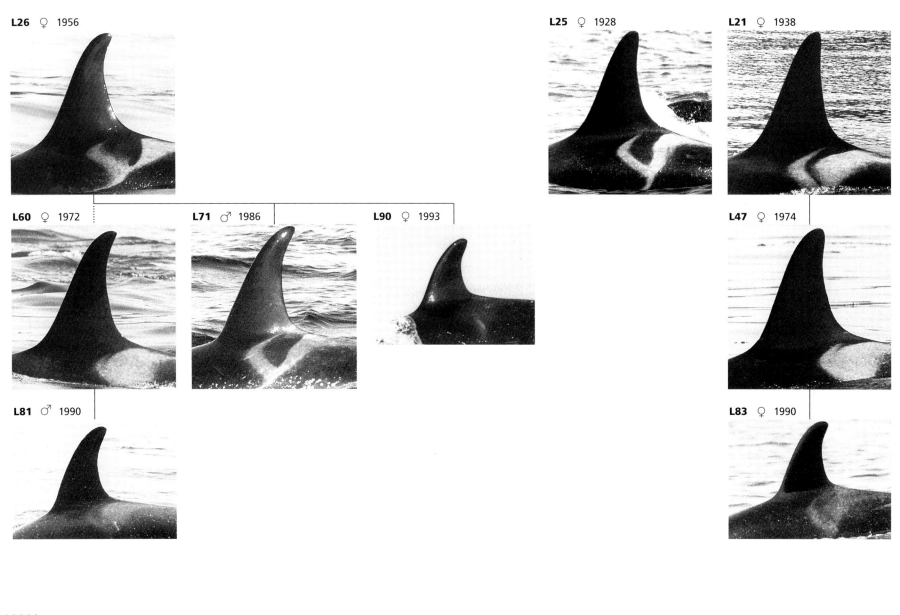

**L26** ♀ 1956

**L60** ♀ 1972

**L71** ♂ 1986

**L90** ♀ 1993

**L81** ♂ 1990

**L25** ♀ 1928

**L21** ♀ 1938

**L47** ♀ 1974

**L83** ♀ 1990

J-Clan

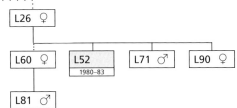

| L26 ♀ | | |
|---|---|---|
| L60 ♀ | L52 | L71 ♂ | L90 ♀ |
|  | 1980–83 | | |
| L81 ♂ | | |

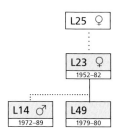

L25 ♀

L23 ♀
1952–82

L14 ♂ | L49
1972–89 | 1979–80

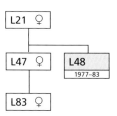

L21 ♀

L47 ♀ | L48
| 1977–83

L83 ♀

# L1 Pod
## L25 Subpod, continued

**L2**  ♀  1945

**L39** ♂ 1975     **L67** 1985     **L78** 1989     **L88** ♂ 1993

**L62** ♂ 1980

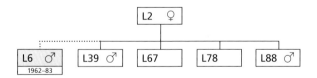

L4 ♀ 1949

L27 ♀ 1965     L61 ♂ 1973     L55 ♀ 1977     L86     1991

L68 ♂ 1985     L80 1990     L82 ♀ 1990

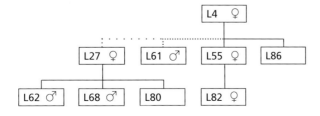

J-Clan

# L1 Pod
## L25 Subpod, continued

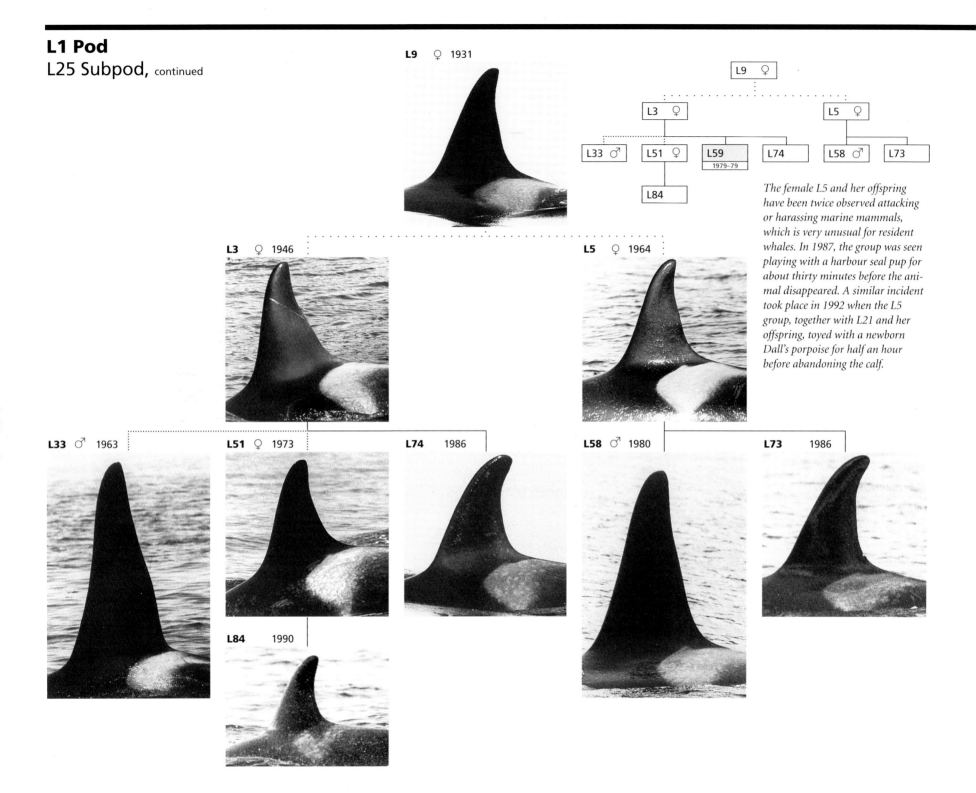

**L9**  ♀  1931

L9  ♀
— L3  ♀
— L33  ♂
— L51  ♀
— L84
— L59 1979–79
— L74
— L5  ♀
— L58  ♂
— L73

*The female L5 and her offspring have been twice observed attacking or harassing marine mammals, which is very unusual for resident whales. In 1987, the group was seen playing with a harbour seal pup for about thirty minutes before the animal disappeared. A similar incident took place in 1992 when the L5 group, together with L21 and her offspring, toyed with a newborn Dall's porpoise for half an hour before abandoning the calf.*

**L3**  ♀  1946

**L5**  ♀  1964

**L33**  ♂  1963

**L51**  ♀  1973

**L74**  1986

**L58**  ♂  1980

**L73**  1986

**L84**  1990

**L45** ♀ 1938

**L57** ♂ 1977

# L1 Pod
## L35 Subpod

**L35** ♀ 1942

*The L35 subpod is the smallest and most independent of the three L subpods. It is seldom seen in the protected "inside" waters without at least one of the other L subpods.*

**L1** ♂ 1959    **L54** ♀ 1977    **L65** ♀ 1984

```
        ┌─────────────┐
        │  L66 ♀      │
        │  1924–86    │
        └─────────────┘
    ┌─────────┐   ┌─────────────┐
    │ L45 ♀   │   │ L8  ♂       │
    └─────────┘   │ 1958–77     │
                  └─────────────┘
┌─────────────┐ ┌─────────┐
│ L36         │ │ L57 ♂   │
│ 1975–75     │ └─────────┘
└─────────────┘
```

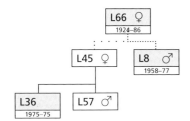

```
            ┌─────────┐
            │ L35 ♀   │
            └─────────┘
┌───────┐ ┌─────────────┐ ┌───────┐ ┌───────┐
│ L1 ♂  │ │ L50 ♂       │ │ L54 ♀ │ │ L65 ♀ │
└───────┘ │ 1973–89     │ └───────┘ └───────┘
          └─────────────┘
```

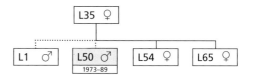

# Afterword

As we finish this book, we are gearing up for the next field season, which, like every previous year, is sure to yield new findings and surprises. Each season, newborn calves are identified, several whales are found to be missing, and interesting patterns of behaviour or social associations are documented. Killer whales are long-lived animals with a relatively low reproductive rate, so it takes many years to build up a good knowledge of their life history and social dynamics. Each additional year of study results in important new data that help us refine our estimates of longevity, birth and death rates, and other vital statistics. Only through long-term research can we fully understand killer whales and protect them and their habitat from potential human impacts.

Once viewed with fear and hostility, killer whales today are regarded with admiration, fascination, respect, and, most important, with a sense of concern for their well-being. More and more, this concern is translating into action. In 1982, public lobbying led to the establishment of the Robson Bight (Michael Bigg) Ecological Reserve, thus protecting important habitat for northern resident whales. More recently, advisory groups, such as the Johnstone Strait Killer Whale Joint Management Committee, have brought together representatives from forestry, fishing, tourism, research, and Native groups to find solutions to local area problems. Whale-watching tour operators in different parts of the coast are in the process of forming associations to establish codes of conduct to minimize whale disturbance. BC Parks has an on-going seasonal warden program at Robson Bight to inform boaters about the Ecological Reserve and that it should not be entered when whales are present. Other education and conservation initiatives include proposals to establish a land-based whale-watching site in the vicinity of Robson Bight, and an interpretive centre for research and education on Johnstone Strait near Telegraph Cove.

In five years or so, we hope to produce another edition of this book with an updated catalogue of resident whales. Many of the individuals shown here will look slightly different, a number will have died, and there will be new additions. We hope to present new findings from our field studies but, above all, we hope to report that the killer whales continue to thrive in the coastal waters of British Columbia and Washington.

# Glossary

The following are definitions of some of the terms used in killer whale research and in this book.

**breach**
occurs when a whale leaps out of the water, exposing two-thirds or more of its body.

**bull**
a sexually mature male; can be identified by its large size and tall dorsal fin, which is at least 1.4 times taller than its width at the base; bulls reach physical maturity at about 20 years of age.

**calf**
a young-of-the-year, typically born in fall-winter.

**clan**
one or more pods that share a related dialect; pods within a clan have probably descended from a common ancestral group and therefore are probably more closely related to each other than to pods from other clans.

**community**
comprises all pods that travel together; pods from different communities have never been seen together.

**cow**
a sexually mature female, usually with at least one offspring; often seen with juveniles following; can be confused with large juvenile males.

**dialect**
a unique set of discrete calls made by an individual whale and fellow pod members; dialects of most resident pods can be distinguished either by ear or with a sound analyzer.

**discrete call**
a type of communication vocalization that sounds the same each time it is produced; on average, resident pods produce about twelve different types of discrete calls.

**echolocation**

the process by which killer whales and other toothed cetaceans use vocalizations to obtain information about their surroundings; similar to SONAR, echolocation involves the production of rapid, high-frequency clicks that echo off objects in the whale's path.

**eye patch**

the elliptically-shaped white patch located above and behind a whale's eye.

**flukes**

the horizontal projections forming the tail of the whale.

**hydrophone**

an underwater microphone used to listen to and record whale vocalizations.

**juvenile**

an immature whale of either sex.

**maternal genealogy**

a family tree showing the ancestry of an individual through its mothers relatives; also known as a matriline.

**matriarch**

the eldest female in a matrilineal group, pod, or subpod.

**matrilineal group**

the basic social unit of resident killer whales, composed of a mature female and her immediate descendants; descendants may include mature males and mature daughters and their offspring.

**offshore killer whales**

a little-known population of killer whales, found mostly in offshore waters off British Columbia; appear to travel in generally larger groups than residents or transients.

**pod**

one or more subpods that usually travel together; term relevant only to resident whales.

**resident killer whales**

a form of killer whales that feeds preferentially on fish, especially salmon, and has a very stable social structure.

**saddle**

the grey pigmented area at the posterior base of the dorsal fin.

**sprouter**

an adolescent male whose fin is undergoing a rapid spurt of growth.

**spyhop**

a behaviour where a whale raises its head vertically above the water, then slips back below the surface; a spyhop seems to be a means of obtaining a view above the surface.

**subpod**

one or more matrilineal groups that temporarily separate as a unit from a pod; members apparently always travel together; term relevant mainly to resident whales.

**transient killer whales**

a form of killer whales that feeds preferentially on marine mammals and has a looser social structure than that of residents; transients also differ from residents in dorsal fin shape, group size, behaviour, and vocalizations.

**whale encounter**

an occasion when one or more identifiable individuals have been located.

The following is a selection of popular and technical articles and books about killer whales, especially in British Columbia and Washington State.

Selected Bibliography

### Popular

Baird, R.W., and Stacey, P.J. 1988. Foraging and feeding behavior of transient killer whales. *Whalewatcher (J. Amer. Cetacean Soc.)* 22:11-15

Balcomb, K.C. 1991. Kith and kin of the killer whale. *Pacific Discovery* 44(2):8-17

Bigg, M.A., Ellis, G., and Balcomb, K.C. 1986. The photographic identification of individual cetaceans. *Whalewatcher (J. Amer. Cetacean Soc.)* 20(2):10-12

Bigg, M.A., Ellis, G.M., Ford, J.K.B., and Balcomb, K.C. 1987. *Killer Whales: A Study of Their Identification, Genealogy and Natural History in British Columbia and Washington State*. Nanaimo, BC: Phantom Press

Bigg, M.A., MacAskie, I.B., and Ellis, G. 1983. Photo-identification of individual killer whales. *Whalewatcher (J. Amer. Cetacean Soc.)* 17(1):3-5

Ford, J.K.B. 1985. Acoustic traditions of killer whales. *Whalewatcher (J. Amer. Cetacean Soc.)* 19(3):3-6

——. 1991. Family fugues. *Natural History* 3:68-76

Ford, J.K.B., and Ford, D. 1981. The killer whales of B.C. *Waters (J. Vancouver Aquarium)* 5(1):1-32

Heise, K., Ellis, G., and Matkin, C. 1991. *A Catalogue of Prince William Sound Killer Whales*. Homer, AK: North Gulf Oceanic Society

Hoyt, E. 1981. *Orca: The Whale Called Killer*. New York, NY: E.P. Dutton

——. 1984. The whales called "killer." *National Geographic* 166(2):220-37

Jeune, P. 1979. *Killer Whale: The Saga of Miracle*. Toronto: McClelland

Matkin, C. 1994. *An Observer's Guide to the Killer Whales of Prince William Sound*. Valdez, AK: Prince William Sound Press

Morton, A. 1991. *Siwiti: A Whale's Story*. Victoria: Orca

——. 1993. *In the Company of Whales*. Victoria: Orca

Obee, B., and Ellis, G. 1992. *Guardians of the Whales*. Vancouver: Whitecap

Osborne, R., Calambokidis, J., and Dorsey, E.M. 1988. *A Guide to Marine Mammals of Greater Puget Sound, including a Catalog of Individual Orca and Minke Whales*. Anacortes, WA: Island Publishers

Sugarman, P. 1984. *Field Guide to the Orca Whales of Greater Puget Sound and Southern British Columbia*. Friday Harbor, WA: The Whale Museum

### Technical

Baird, R.W., and Stacey, P.J. 1988. Variation in saddle patch pigmentation in populations of killer whale (*Orcinus orca*) from British Columbia, Alaska and Washington State. *Can. J. Zool.* 66:2582-85

Balcomb, K.C., Boran, J.R., and Heimlich, S.L. 1982. Killer whales in Greater Puget Sound. *Rep. Int. Whal. Commn.* 32:681-85

Bigg, M.A., Olesiuk, P.F., Ellis, G.M., Ford, J.K.B., and Balcomb, K.C., III. 1990. Social organization and genealogy of resident killer whales (*Orcinus orca*) in the coastal waters of British Columbia and Washington State. *Rep. Int. Whal. Commn.*, Special Issue 12, 383-405

Bigg, M.A., and Wolman, A.A. 1976. Live-capture killer whale (*Orcinus orca*) fishery, British Columbia and Washington State, 1962-72. *J. Fish. Res. Bd Can.* 32:1213-21

Felleman, F.L., Heimlich-Boran, J.R., and Osborne, R.W. 1991. The feeding ecology of killer whales (*Orcinus orca*) in the Pacific northwest. In K. Pryor and K.S. Norris (eds.), *Dolphin Societies: Discoveries and Puzzles* (pp. 113-47). Berkeley: University of California Press

Ford, J.K.B. 1987. A catalogue of underwater calls produced by killer whales (*Orcinus orca*) in British Columbia. *Can. Data Rep. Fish. Aquat. Sci.* (No. 633), 165 pp.

——. 1989. Acoustic behaviour of resident killer whales (*Orcinus orca*) off Vancouver Island, British Columbia. *Can. J. Zool.* 67:727-45

——. 1991. Vocal traditions among resident killer whales (*Orcinus orca*) in coastal waters of British Columbia. *Can. J. Zool.* 69:1454-83

Heimlich-Boran, J.R. 1988. Behavioral ecology of killer whales (*Orcinus orca*) in the Pacific Northwest. *Can. J. Zool.* 66:565-78

Heyning, J.E., and Dahlheim, M.E. 1988. *Orcinus Orca.* Mammalian Species 304. *Amer. Soc. Mammologists* 15 (January):1-9

Jefferson, T.A., Stacey, P.J., and Baird, R.W. 1991. A review of killer whale interactions with other marine mammals: predation to co-existence. *Mar. Rev.* 21:151-180

Kirkevold, B.C., and Lockard, J.S. (eds.). 1986. *Behavioral Biology of Killer Whales.* New York, NY: Alan R. Liss

Nichol, L.M. 1990. Seasonal movements and foraging behaviour of resident killer whales (*Orcinus orca*) in relation to the inshore distribution of salmon (*Oncorhynchus* spp.) in British Columbia. M.Sc. Thesis, University of British Columbia, Vancouver, BC

Olesiuk, P.F., Bigg, M.A., and Ellis, G.M. 1990. Life history and population dynamics of resident killer whales (*Orcinus orca*) in the coastal waters of British Columbia and Washington State. *Rep. Int. Whal. Commn.*, Special Issue 12, 209-43

## Videos

*Island of Whales.* National Film Board, Vancouver, 1989
*Killer Whales: Wolves of the Sea.* National Geographic Society, 1993
These films contain accurate natural history information and scenes of killer whales in British Columbia and other regions. They are available on videotape from the sources shown or from the Vancouver Aquarium, P.O. Box 3232, Vancouver, BC V6B 3X8.

## Sound Recordings

*Blackfish Sound: Underwater Communication of Killer Whales in British Columbia.* Vancouver Aquarium Research 1992.
This recording features examples of pod dialects and vocalizations recorded during various activities of resident killer whales. It is available in CD or audio-cassette formats from the Vancouver Aquarium (address above) or from Holborne Distributing Co. Ltd., P.O. Box 309S, Mt. Albert, Ontario L0G 1M0.

## Whale Adoption Programs

Programs to symbolically adopt whales are an interesting and popular way for people to learn about killer whales. At the same time, they provide funding for field research and conservation. Proceeds from the following two adoption programs directly support the annual photo-identification studies described in this book.

*For northern resident and transient killer whales, contact:*
Killer Whale Adoption Program
Vancouver Aquarium
P.O. Box 3232
Vancouver, BC V6B 3X8
Phone: (604) 631-2516; fax: (604) 631-2529

*For southern resident killer whales, contact:*
Orca Adoption Program,
The Whale Museum
P.O. Box 945
Friday Harbor, WA 98250
Phone: (206) 378-4710; fax: (206) 378-5790

## Research, Conservation, and Education Organizations

The following organizations have programs in research, conservation, or public education involving killer whales.

*British Columbia:*
BC Parks, Strathcona District
Rathtrevor Beach Park
Parksville, BC V0R 2S0

Johnstone Strait Killer Whale Interpretive Centre Society
P.O. Box 3
Telegraph Cove, BC V0N 3J0

Marine Mammal Research Group
P.O. Box 6244
Victoria, BC V8P 5L5
Phone: (604) 380-1925; fax: (604) 380-1206
Whale Sighting and Stranding Report Line (BC only): 1-800-665-5939

Orcalab
P.O. Box 258
Alert Bay, BC V0N 1A0

Pacific Biological Station
Department of Fisheries and Oceans
Nanaimo, BC V9R 5K6
Phone: (604) 756-7245; fax: (604) 756-7053

Raincoast Research
Simoom Sound, BC V0P 1S0

Sidney Museum
2440 Sidney Avenue
Sidney, BC V8L 1Y7
Phone: (604) 656-1322; fax: (604) 655-4508

UBC Marine Mammal Research Unit
Fisheries Centre
University of British Columbia
Vancouver, BC V6T 1Z4
Phone: (604) 822-8181; fax: (604) 822-8180

University of Victoria Department of Geography
University of Victoria
Victoria, BC V8W 2Y2
Phone: (604) 721-7344; fax: (604) 721-6216

Vancouver Aquarium
P.O. Box 3232
Vancouver, BC V6B 3X8
Phone: (604) 685-3364; fax: (604) 631-2529

West Coast Whale Research Foundation
2020-1040 West Georgia Street
Vancouver, BC V6E 4H1
Phone: (604) 731-2166

*Washington:*
Center for Whale Research
P.O. Box 1577
Friday Harbor, WA 98250
Phone: (206) 378-5835; fax: (206) 378-5954

The Whale Museum
P.O. Box 945
Friday Harbor, WA 98250
Phone: (206) 378-4710; fax: (206) 378-5790
Whale Sighting and Stranding Report Line (Washington only): 1-800-562-8832

Other
Resources

## Photographic Credits

We are grateful to the friends and colleagues who have contributed photographs for this book. They are listed below.

| page | photographer |
| --- | --- |
| 2 | John Ford |
| 6 | Kelley Balcomb-Bartok |
| 10 | John Ford |
| 15 | Kelley Balcomb-Bartok |
| 19 (top) | Lance Barrett-Lennard |
| 19 (bottom) | John Ford |
| 20 (top) | Jim Borrowman |
| 20 (bottom, left) | Karl Solomon |
| 20 (bottom, right) | Gorden Schweers |
| 22 | John Ford |
| 26 | Craig Matkin |
| 28 (top) | John Ford |
| 28 (bottom) | Graeme Ellis |
| 32 (top) | Graeme Ellis |
| 32 (bottom) | John Ford |
| 33 | Graeme Ellis |
| 34 | Elizabeth Parer-Cook |
| 35 (top, bottom) | Kelley Balcomb-Bartok |
| 36 (top) | Graeme Ellis |
| 36 (bottom) | John Ford |
| 37 | John Ford |
| 38 | Kelley Balcomb-Bartok |
| 39 (top) | John Ford |
| 39 (bottom) | Graeme Ellis |
| 40 | Graeme Ellis |
| 42 (bottom) | Ian MacAskie |
| 44 (top) | David Ellifrit |
| 44 (bottom) | Graeme Ellis |
| 48 | Graeme Ellis |
| 53 | Graeme Ellis |
| 77 | John Ford |

| catalogue photographs | photographer | number of photos |
| --- | --- | --- |
| Northern resident whales | Graeme Ellis | 162 |
| | John Ford | 39 |
| | Alexandra Morton | 7 |
| | John De Boeck | 1 |
| Southern resident whales | Ken Balcomb | 24 |
| | Astrid van Ginnekan | 24 |
| | David Ellifrit | 20 |
| | Diane Claridge | 8 |
| | Prentice Bloedel | 2 |
| | Jim Boehmer | 2 |
| | Curt Jenner | 2 |
| | Karen Birbeck | 1 |
| | Gundel Bowen | 1 |
| | Jenny Cuccinello | 1 |
| | John Durban | 1 |
| | Paul Ellifrit | 1 |
| | Jude Forster | 1 |
| | Kevin Hobbs | 1 |
| | William Jochimsen | 1 |
| | Ann Malys | 1 |
| | Marilyn Martino | 1 |
| | Stephanie Ralph | 1 |
| | Ed Soule | 1 |
| | Arthur Teranishi | 1 |
| | Kate Whitacre | 1 |

Set in Minion, Frutiger, and Univers
Designer: George Vaitkunas
Copy-editor: Holly Keller-Brohman
Printed and bound in Canada by D.W. Friesen & Sons Ltd.